Discovering
BODMIN MOOR

E. V. Thompson

BOSSINEY BOOKS

First published in 1980
by Bossiney Books
St Teath, Bodmin, Cornwall
Typeset and printed in Great Britain by
Penwell Ltd, Parkwood, Callington
Cornwall

ISBN O 906456 40 1

PLATE ACKNOWLEDGMENTS

Cover photograph by Murray King
Map by Paul Honeywill
page 100 Murray King
page 44 Bryan Russell
page 15 David Clarke
All other photographs by Ray Bishop

ABOUT THE AUTHOR

E.V. Thompson, who was born in London, lived for some years in an old miner's cottage on Bodmin Moor. He and his family and animals now live near Pentewan. He spent nine years in the Navy before joining the Bristol Police Force where he was a founder member of the Vice Squad. Then he worked as an investigator with B.O.A.C., with the Hong Kong Police Narcotics Bureau — and was later Chief Security Officer of Rhodesia's Department of Civil Aviation.

On returning to England he set out to be a full-time professional writer. A year later, broke but still writing, he swept factory floors. Then in 1977 his first book *Chase the Wind* won the 'Best Historical Novel Competition' and became a bestseller. This novel, set on the beautiful but brooding moors of Bodmin, has been followed by two others, both published by Macmillan.

Here, in his debut for Bossiney, E.V. Thompson returns to the theme of his great Cornish love: Bodmin Moor. 'To strike out across the coarse grass, leaving behind the grey stone moorside hamlets, is to stride back into history,' he says. 'Almost every age of man has left its brief mark here. From the grass-covered mound of a Bronze Age hut, to a furrow carved by a crashing American aircraft during World War II.'

Discovering Bodmin Moor is absolutely the right title, for here the author encourages us to do precisely that.

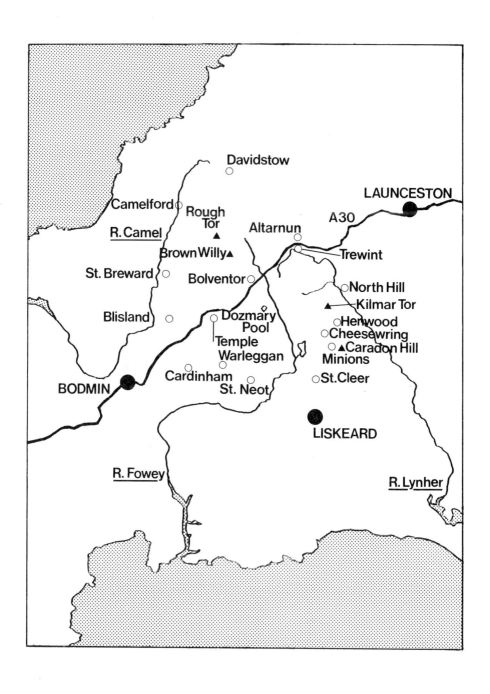

Discovering
BODMIN
MOOR

There is something indefinably romantic about a large tract of beautiful, windswept countryside, rich in history and legend, lying empty and almost unknown in the middle of England's most popular holiday county. Especially if that stretch of land is being gradually eroded by progress.

Bodmin Moor is just such a place. It has been at the heart of all that is Cornwall since man made his first primitive home here almost 7,000 years ago. For the visitor with sufficient time, and the interest to seek it out, history lies on every rocky tor, and lurks in each lonely valley, side-by-side with romance and legend.

Yet, in spite of this, mention Bodmin Moor to a summer holiday-maker at one of the coastal towns or villages and he or she will probably reply, 'Oh yes! We have seen it. We drove across the moor on our way here.'

There can be few visitors to Cornwall who have *not* seen this expanse of granite upland. Approached from the east, its dark heights dominate the horizon.

The rugged, boulder-strewn tors have changed little over the centuries. Stone Age man; Roman trader; Dark Age Saint; Saxon Chieftain; Norman Earl; Medieval farmer — even King Arthur himself — would feel at home were they to return to the heart of the moor today. This sense of timelessness is felt by all who come to know and love Bodmin Moor.

To strike out across the coarse grass, leaving behind the grey stone moorside hamlets, is to stride back into history. Almost every age of man has left its brief mark here. From the grass-covered mound of a Bronze Age hut, to the furrow carved by a crashing American aircraft during World War II.

EARLY DAYS

When Bodmin Moor's history began, most of Cornwall was covered with dense forest. Only a few coastal areas and the high moor were unwooded. With his indifferent tools and primitive weapons, Stone Age man was unable to clear the lowland undergrowth where he was at the mercy of wild animals — and his fellow men. He moved inland, to the hills of Bodmin Moor.

One such early dwelling-site is on the shores of Dozmary Pool. This dark, brooding, reed-fringed basin of water, a mile in circumference, lies about 900 feet above sea level. Dozmary Pool is woven into the fabric of the moor, factually and in legend. It will receive more than one mention in this narrative.

On the shores of the pool, where deer came to drink until comparatively recent times, Stone Age man left many of his flint-flake microliths for us to find. Inserted in a stick, these tiny, chipped blades of stone were used by our ancestors as both tools and a means of hunting. It was a flimsy weapon with which to bring down a deer — and little defence against an enraged boar, but it served him for many centuries.

Progress was slow in this period of prehistory and Stone Age man fought his tenacious battle for survival on Bodmin Moor for 2,000 years before a new and advanced Stone Age man reached Cornwall from the continent of Europe. Although he too used implements of stone, the newcomer was far in advance of the man he found here. He had learned to make efficient stone axes and with these was able to clear large areas of the lowland forest. In these man-made clearings he tilled the land, grew food and grazed cattle and sheep. When he went hunting he took with him dogs to harry his prey and lessen the danger to himself.

These new Stone Age residents of Britain were the builders of Stonehenge, on the downs of Wiltshire. Here, on Bodmin Moor, they provided us with one of Cornwall's oldest man-made monuments, the Stripple Stones on the slopes of Hawk's Tor, just north of the A30 road. This should not be confused with the tor of the same name rising above Trebartha, on the eastern moor.

Only four of the stones now remain from this ancient henge where

Dozmary Pool: 'woven into the fabric of the Moor.' ▶

once there was a stone circle with surrounding ditch and bank. Many of the stones from the henge were used to make the field hedge which now intrudes upon the site.

Linking the Stone Age with the Bronze Age were the 'Beaker Folk', who reached the moor somewhere around 2,000 BC. Originating in Spain, the Beaker Folk were so-called because of their habit of burying small beakers with their dead. Traders and voyagers, they had an elementary knowledge of metal working, and copper knives have been found in their graves.

The Beaker Folk coincide with the Megalithic period of history, to which we owe a number of Bodmin Moor's better known ancient monuments. The Hurlers, on the edge of Minions village, and the Nine Stones, just off East Moor, are but two examples of the many stone circles built around 1,500 BC.

The Hurlers are the remains of three stone circles and owe their name to the legend that they were once men, turned to stone for playing the old Cornish game of 'hurling' on a Sunday. Many reasons for these circles have been advanced. They were for religious purposes; sacrificial rites; meeting-places, with one stone for each tribal or community leader . . . the speculation is unending. Whatever the reason, it must have taken the combined efforts of a great many men to drag some of these huge stones across the moorland and raise them into position. Perhaps the truth is to be found somewhere on the moor, awaiting discovery.

Less of a mystery are the stone tombs, or cromlechs, erected at about the same time. They consist of a number of large, upright, flat rocks upon which is placed an even larger capstone to create a huge tomb. Originally they would have had earth piled about them, but time and man have removed much of the earth.

A magnificent example of such a tomb is Trethevy Quoit, near Tremar, in the parish of St Cleer. The viewer cannot fail to be impressed by the skill and determination of the men who erected such an impressive and enduring resting-place for one of their own.

Cornwall was now in the Bronze Age, and the discovery that tin and copper together produced the much tougher bronze gave Bodmin Moor an economic importance that would last until the

Sharptor: 'from here one has a breathtaking view of the whole of East Cornwall.' ▶

Roughtor: 'an enduring memorial to the 43rd Wessex Division.'

early years of the the twentieth century, for the moor has both tin and copper ores.

Bronze Age man has left us with many examples of his manner of life — and death. A member of a very well-organised society, he had trade links that extended from Ireland to the Mediterranean. He was a communal man, living in a village, or small community unit, each with its chieftain, or petty ruler. The remains of these communities are scattered the length and breadth of Bodmin Moor, as a glance at one of the Ordnance maps will show. Few of these sites have been excavated and they have always been utilised as a handy source of stone for walls and animal shelters. Fortunately, those on the Duchy of Cornwall farms, at least, have been given a degree of protection. The Duchy forbids tenant farmers to disturb these sites.

From the huge number of hut circles remaining today, it is apparent that in the Bronze Age Bodmin Moor was far more heavily populated than it is today.

Most of these ancient 'villages' are on the slopes of the tors, some being of considerable size. One large group sprawls along the slopes of Langstone Downs, above the Withybrook Marsh. Another, far more compact and with even more huts, occupies a hillside at Blacktor Downs, just south of the A30 turn-off to Temple. No doubt a number of the sites shown on the map belong to the later Iron Age, but this can only be determined by excavation.

One of the most archaeologically exciting features of Early Bronze Age culture was their habit of burying their chieftains in barrows, accompanied by many of their worldly possessions — and sometimes by members of their family and household. As gold was known to Bronze Age man, many of his tombs have been looted by fortune-seekers. Nevertheless, there are a great many known barrows on Bodmin Moor and, doubtless, many more have yet to be discovered.

Close to Minions village, on the lower slopes of the hill upon which stands the Cheesewring, is a barrow that was partially excavated by

The Prince of Wales shaft at the Phoenix Mine.

a group of miners in 1836, or 1837. Set in the side of the barrow they found a stone tomb. Inside were the remains of a skeleton, together with beads, pottery, a dagger and a small, ribbed gold cup of a type that has also been found in tombs at Mycenae, an ancient Greek city.

Known as the Rillaton Cup, this priceless relic was presented to William IV. After the death of the eccentric and jovial 'sailor-king', a search was made for the gold cup. It was eventually discovered in the royal bathroom — where it had seen service as a shaving-mug. The Rillaton Cup is now in the British Museum, in London. A replica may be seen in the County Museum, Truro.

The Bronze Age lasted for almost 1,300 years. During this time change came slowly to our primitive ancestors. They tended their sheep and cattle, tilled the land and slowly improved their bronze tools. Their arsenal of weapons-of-war also increased. In addition to bow and arrow and bronze-tipped spear, the Bronze Age warrior now had the sword. No doubt the idea was given to him by one of the many travellers who crossed the moor. Cornwall was on the important trade route between Ireland — rich in gold and copper — and the cultural centres of the Mediterranean.

During the latter years of the Bronze Age there was an ever-increasing flow of Celtic settlers to the country from Europe. Not unnaturally, a number found their way to Cornwall and were assimilated into the community.

Then, sometime during the fifth century BC a new kind of Celtic immigrant arrived on these shores. Warlike and quarrelsome, the new breed of Celtic warriors had learned the use of iron and utilised their knowledge to manufacture more sophisticated weapons than their predecessors. Armed with these, they set out to conquer most of Central and Western Europe.

This was the people who brought to Cornwall the language that survives to this day.

A warlike race, these early Celts soon found it necessary to protect their newly-won territory against fellow-Celts who came after. They built the hill-forts that can be seen today on many of the hilltops around the edge of the moor.

One of the most easily accessible sites — and certainly the one

◀ **Bearah Tor on the eastern edge of the Moor.**

13

most evocative of the past — is on the summit of Stowe's Hill, alongside the balancing rocks of the Cheesewring. The stones of the perimeter walls are heaped upon each other to form a huge, defensive pound, making clever use of the natural contours of the hill. Where it is less steep, a double defence has been built.

Such precautions were necessary, for by now the threat to the Celts of Cornwall from their fellow-tribesmen living across the River Tamar was a very real one.

Come to this spot alone on a crisp winter's day and you will have a view of the whole plain of the Tamar River, from Dartmoor to Bodmin Moor. Its strategic value is immediately apparent. Sit here a while and your thoughts slip back in time. How often must this steep hillside have rung to the clash of Iron Age weapons and the cries of warring men? No one knows the answer. No excavations have taken place here to uncover the secrets of the past.

There are many such defensive fortresses around the edge of the moor. Berry Down, north east of St Neot village, and Bury Castle at Cardinham are but two. The Iron Age Celts were also farming men. Unless there was the threat of imminent danger they preferred to farm the more fertile lowlands. Nevertheless, many of them did settle the moor and managed successfully to farm the uplands.

On Garrow Tor there is a most interesting archaeological site which has been partly excavated. Evidence has been found to establish that an Iron Age settlement was built upon a Bronze Age site and the occupation continued through Saxon times and well into the Middle Ages.

THE ROMANS

During the first century BC the Romans sent two of their armies into England, but they were punitive expeditions only. Rome had no designs on the British Isles at this time, and for almost a hundred years afterwards the only contact between Rome and Celtic Britain came through trade.

The Celts changed little over the years. They remained as

The Author and son, Nathan — a Sharptor baby. ▶

Brown Willy — the highest point in Cornwall.

quarrelsome as they had always been. Grouped in larger tribal units now, with chieftains who called themselves 'Kings', they waged murderous war on their neighbours at the slightest provocation.

The Romans, who now occupied much of Europe, decided the time had arrived to subdue their squabbling northern neighbours. In AD 43, the Roman general Aulus Plautius landed in Kent. The conquest of England had begun.

For a great many years it was believed by historians that the conquering Roman armies never crossed west of the Tamar. While it is true that the early Roman occupation had little effect upon Cornwall — and in particular upon the residents of Cornwall's high moor, there is now ample evidence that at some time after they had subdued the remainder of the country, the Roman legions forded the Tamar River and carried their eagles among the tribes of Cornwall — The Dumnonii. The Romans succeeded in isolating the Cornish Celts from their kinsmen in South Wales and from this time Cornwall began to develop in its own way.

The Romans made no attempt to permanently occupy Cornwall.

There was nothing here of interest to them. There was tin, of course, but they obtained theirs from Spain, a land closer to the heart of the Roman world.

But, although Rome did not colonise the county, every nation has its pioneers and in the exciting days of expanding empire Rome had no shortage of such men. Many enterprising Romans made their way into Cornwall, passing over the open land of the high moor. A stranger in a new and still savage land, he would have felt safer on high ground, where a potential enemy could be sighted when still many miles away.

Most of Rome's traders arrived in Cornwall from the sea and a few headed inland never to return. Huge finds of coins close to good landing sites tend to confirm this. Perhaps the owner of the 2,500 coins discovered at Caerhays, on the coast close to Gorran Haven, was one such trader. If any reached Bodmin Moor they left behind no recognisable Roman dwelling as proof of their visit.

However, there were a number of enterprising military leaders stationed at the great Roman outposts of Caerleon, in South Wales, and at Exeter. From here centurions were sent out with their companies of soldiers to explore the wild country of the Western Celts. It is certain that these sons of Imperial Rome tramped the turf of the moor. Their route would have taken them across the River Tamar, at the spot where Horsebridge now stands, through Linkinhorne parish and across the ancient track that rose steadily in the shadow of Caradon, until it passed the ancient stone circles of The Hurlers.

On Goonzion Down beyond St Neot village is an earthwork where it is believed Roman soldiers erected some form of temporary defensive camp. A few miles away, just off the moor at Nanstallon, is another earthwork. Excavations have shown that this site was occupied by Roman soldiers for almost a quarter of a century during the earlier years of the Roman conquest. A number of the interesting finds made may be seen in Bodmin museum. The historian Fortescue Hitchins, writing early in the nineteenth century, repeats the local tradition that a whole Roman Legion — between 3,000 and 6,000 men — was once stationed at Liskeard. Unfortunately, no evidence has been found to support this belief.

As the strength of Rome ebbed away, envious nations began to probe the strength and weaknesses of her extended borders. About the year 250 AD, Rome lost her supply of tin from Spain. Suddenly

Cornwall's tin mines resumed some of the importance they had known in earlier years, and which they would retain for many centuries. Much of the tin trade was carried on by sea routes, but it was of sufficient importance for the Romans to push roads through the county to carry out the tin ore, or smelted tin ingots. Milestones, or more accurately stones dedicated to the emperor who reigned when a road was built, have been found in north and west Cornwall. In addition to the road from Horsebridge, one of the major routes would have cut across the heart of the moor, tracing the route now followed by modern travellers along the A30.

After three and a half centuries of Roman occupation and protection, the people of England and Wales now regarded themselves as Roman citizens. It came as a great shock when the fast-crumbling Empire of Rome announced that it was withdrawing its legions from Britain. But, in 410 AD that is exactly what happened.

THE DARK AGES

The dismayed country that the Romans left behind was quickly plunged into the 'Dark Ages' and invasion followed invasion as Angles, Saxons and Danes fought for a foothold in the unprotected land that had shattered into numerous small and weak 'kingdoms'.

Thirty years after the Romans had left the country, a pathetic plea for help was sent to Rome by the Britons, 'The barbarians drive us into the sea, the sea drives us back on to the barbarians. Our only choice is whether we shall die by the sword, or drown, for we have none to save us.'

At first the plight of their countrymen mattered little to the Cornish Celts. They had no towns, cities, or even rich mansion houses to attract the invader. The people lived much as they had since before the Romans came. Their crude stone houses and isolated villages were hardly worthy of the attentions of a plundering army. There *were* raids, but these were on coastal communities. Inland, on the high moor, life went on much as before.

Sharptor: 'my favourite tor and easily accessible.' ▶

Then the land west of the Tamar witnessed the arrival of a new breed of settler — the men and women who were followers of Christ. Christians. The first to arrive would have been refugees from the east, driven from their homes by the barbarian Saxon and beaten steadily westwards until they found refuge in the hills of Wales and the unknown lands of the Cornish Dumnonii.

It was indeed ironic that here where Roman influence had been least felt, the flame of Roman Christianity should burn so strongly. Elsewhere in Britain it had been brutally extinguished.

Throughout more than five centuries of the Dark Ages, Christianity was carefully nurtured in Cornwall as the early Saints and mystics crossed and re-crossed the moor. Travelling between Europe, Wales and Ireland, Cornwall was safer for them than the sea route around Land's End and unless a Saint had an ambition to become a martyr he did not venture eastward to where the Saxon now dominated the whole land.

Many of these early Saints remained in Cornwall, some for only a short while, others for all their lives. Bodmin Moor was popular with these holy men and women. Seeking solitude, a place where they might find communion with their God, the places they settled are marked on the map of Cornwall for all to see. St Tudy; St Clether; St Neot; St Cleer — and of course, Altarnon, the 'Altar of St Non (or Nonna)'.

This good lady was the mother of St David of Wales and more than one historian has suggested that St David himself was in fact a Cornishman, born here, at Altarnon, now usually spelt Altarnun. The cross that stands at the entrance to the present church dates from the sixth century, when St Nonna prayed here. Her well was long famed for curing unfortunates afflicted with madness. They were dunked in the well until, half-drowned and almost insensible, they were carried to the church and pronounced 'cured'.

From this hazy period of history we have a wealth of legend concerning the Saints. In those days saintliness must have been a family business. One Brychen of Wales who settled here is reputed to have had twelve sons and twelve daughters. Each of them becoming a 'Saint'!

These holy men and women continued to arrive in Cornwall

Sixth century cross in Altarnon Churchyard. ▶

throughout the whole of the Dark Ages, many making a lasting impression upon their adopted county. This is not surprising when we learn they many of them are reported as living to incredible ages. St Piran, patron Saint of Cornish tinners, holds the record. He is said to have lived for 200 years after reaching Cornwall.

St Neot did not arrive until the latter half of the ninth century and is believed to have been a Saxon and not a Celt. Most accounts suggest he was a close kinsman of King Alfred, who reigned from 871 to 901 AD. It is fairly certain that Alfred visited St Neot during his reign and was cured of a sickness by this Saint. There are a great many legends about St Neot and such was his love of animals, he can lay claim to being Cornwall's own 'Francis of Assisi'.

The legends of this age are not restricted to the lives of the Saints. This is the time — and the place — for the emergence of the legendary King Arthur, the best known, yet least authenticated of Celtic Kings. There can be few monarchs, real or fictional, who have had more written about them than King Arthur and his fabled 'Knights of the Round Table'. All this — and it must be said — without a fragment of *real* evidence that such a man ever existed!

Having made such a bold statement, I hasten to add that the Dark Ages produced little documentary evidence of any description. *I* do not doubt for one moment that such a king lived, or that he rode Cornwall's moor on his journeys from Camelot (Camelford?).

Here on Bodmin Moor those who seek Arthurian associations will find King Arthur's Hall, King Arthur's Bed and King Arthur's Downs. They will doubtless visit Dozmary Pool, where only the most hardened sceptic could doubt that the dark waters of this moorland lake once closed over the mighty sword 'Excalibur' as a King died and a legend was born. It was a legend that would gain strength with every passing year.

Of more solid substance than Dark Age legend are the granite inscribed stones of this era, left behind as long-enduring memorials to Kings whose reigns were brief, their achievements long-forgotten.

In Lewannick churchyard, two such stones were discovered in the last century, inscribed with both Latin and the 'Ogham' script, which has its origins in Ireland. A stone at Slaughter Bridge near

◀ **Arthur being offered Excalibur by the Lady of the Lake — painting by W. Hatherell.**

Dozmary Pool: 'where the legend of the sword ended.'

Camelford also carries both scripts. This stone is known as King Arthur's tomb, but the Irish associations tend to make the more romantic remember the haunting legend of Tristan and Iseult.

Another stone may be seen in St Cleer parish, beside the Redgate — Minions Road. The inscription, carved in Latin, tells us that the monument was erected for the soul of King Doniert. One of the last of the Cornish Kings, Doniert was drowned in the nearby River Fowey in 878 AD. Standing at this lonely, roadside memorial, looking out across the moorland, it is interesting to speculate upon the extent of King Doniert's kingdom in those far-off days. How many subjects did he rule? What manner of men were they? One thing we do know. Doniert would have needed to be a warrior King. The Saxons had by now adopted Christianity, but they showed little Christian charity towards their neighbours.

Throughout the latter years of the Dark Ages the Saxons fought to gain ascendency over the Dumnonii of Cornwall. It was a see-saw affair. During the eighth and ninth centuries, battles between the

24

Inscribed stone at Slaughter Bridge known as Arthur's tomb.

two opposing forces were fought on both sides of the River Tamar. The tribes of Cornwall frequently called for assistance from the Danes, who were harrying the Saxons in the north and east of England.

In 814 AD the Saxons ravaged the county from end to end. A great battle was fought in 823 AD but historians are divided as to whether this took place in Devon, or at Slaughter Bridge, close to Camelford. It is certain that a battle did take place at Slaughter Bridge sometime during the Dark Ages, but there are many who prefer to believe it was fought between the forces of King Arthur and his nephew Mordred. The site fits in neatly with much of the Arthurian legend. Carried dying from the battlefield, King Arthur would have been within sight of his city of Camelot and only a few miles from Dozmary Pool where Sir Bedivere hurled the King's sword.

In 838 AD the Saxons inflicted a crushing defeat on the combined Cornish-Danish army. The battle was fought on Hingston Down,

25

just a few miles east of Bodmin Moor. Yet, although the battle proved so decisive, Cornwall was able to keep its own Kings and did not come under full Saxon domination for another hundred years.

It was in 931 AD that Athelstan, after subduing unruly elements in Cornwall, created a diocese of Cornwall with its Bishop in St Germans. Here for the first time we have the original version of the county's present name. 'Cornewalas' was the Saxon name and gives us an indication of the feelings of the Saxons for the Celts. The name comes from the Saxon word meaning 'strangers'. Athelstan had learned that the Cornish possessed an identity of their own!

As Cornwall began to emerge from the Dark Ages we obtain a clearer picture of life on Bodmin Moor. There were far fewer people here now than during the late Bronze and Iron Ages. The climate had slowly deteriorated, making the moor a bleak and exposed area. Most of its inhabitants had moved to more hospitable regions around the fringe of the moor, but there were still a few communities who clung tenaciously to their hardy way of life on this high granite plateau.

On Garrow Tor, the centuries-old community continued to farm, sharing their homes with their animals, gathering peat for fires to keep out the cold of the winter mists, and growing sparse crops.

The people here spoke the ancient Celtic language and not the Anglo-Saxon of their overlords. This alone was sufficient to ensure that they remained — 'The Strangers'.

The manors that became established around the fringes of the moor held much of the moorland between them, with tenants tilling the land and slaves tending the animals. Religious houses at Launceston, Bodmin and St Neot also had impressive land-holdings.

Throughout the years of Anglo-Saxon rule the monasteries grabbed more and more of the countryside. King Cnut 'The Canute of tidal fame' gave many grants of land to the Cathedral Church of St Germans during his reign, including tracts of Bodmin Moor. From the documents confirming these grants we are given a picture of the countryside as it was then. The borders of one such grant in 1018 AD follow the moorland River Lynher for a way, takes a line to a well, mentions a couple of burial mounds (barrows), follows a field wall, mentions a fire-cleft tree-stump, etc. King Cnut was also a very careful man when he made his grants. His documents were couched in flowery Latin, praising the King for his generosity and good works, but when it came to describing boundaries, the wording was in plain, simple Anglo-Saxon to ensure there was no mistaking its meaning.

THE MEDIEVAL MOOR

Some parts of the moor were kept in Royal hands — as, indeed, much of it is today. Prior to the Norman conquest, the manor of Blisland was held by King Harold. With the arrival of the Normans, Bodmin Moor received a new lease of life. Almost the whole of Cornwall was given to Robert, Count of Mortain. Half-brother to William the Conqueror, Robert became the wealthiest man in England after the King.

In order to keep the lands he had been given, Robert built a number of castle strongholds in the county and strengthened others, including Launceston — Launceston had served both Celt and Saxon as a stronghold. Another of Robert's castles was at Cardinham, held for him there by his steward, Richard FitzTurold. This castle stood for 300 years, but little remains now but the faintest of outlines.

Within a few years the whole of Cornwall was in Norman hands and only a handful of tenants were either Saxon or Celt. The change in landowners affected only those who had been dispossessed. For the Celtic speaking serfs the conquest meant little. Serf or villein, call them what you will, they were no more than slaves — only now their orders were shouted at them in French.

There were greater changes in store for the monasteries. Few of them came up to the high standards set by the Normans — and William needed an excuse to bring the not inconsiderable wealth and power of the Church into Norman hands. Launceston Priory was suppressed and a new priory built for Augustinian priors in the early twelfth century. Bodmin Priory suffered a similar fate, while the small monastery of St Neot was closed altogether.

The Normans also went in for a great deal of church building and re-building. A new one was built at Altarnon to take the place of St Nonna's church, built six hundred years before. Nothing was left but the ancient stone cross to remind us of that Dark Age building. Later still another church took the place of the Norman house of

worship and we have only the font, a piscina bowl and shaft, and a scrap of a pillar to hint at its former glory.

Blisland church has retained more of its Norman architecture. Nestling beside the village green, the church gives the casual visitor no hint of the beauty to be found inside — albeit that much of the beauty is provided by woodwork much younger than the Norman period.

When Robert of Mortain's son joined a rebellion against the King, it was swiftly put down, but it brought about a general redistribution of the tenancies of Cornwall's manors. It was probably at this time that the manor of Trebartha, set in a beautiful valley near North Hill, was given to the Norman who took the name of Trebartha for his own (see under 'North Hill').

Now that Cornwall was under the effective control of the English Crown, there was an influx of settlers to Bodmin Moor and many of today's farms can trace their origins to this period.

Left: Altarnon Church 'at the heart of a most pleasing Cornish village.'
Below: Blisland with its green is untypical of a Cornish village.

Temple, just off the main A30 trunk road, owes its name to the hospice founded here as a refuge for pilgrims and travellers, en route to the Holy Land. No doubt a number of Pilgrims to the Middle East did set off from the safe ports and harbours of Cornwall, but it is far more likely that many of the pilgrims made their way across the moor to visit the priory at Bodmin — where were housed the bones of St Petroc, said to perform miracles for the faithful — or to the Abbey on St Michael's Mount.

An enchanting island at high tide, St Michael's Mount claimed to hold even more for the believer. On this impressive rock St Michael himself had appeared to fishermen, whilst in the abbey there were a number of bizarre relics, including the sacred milk of the Blessed Virgin Mary, stones from the sepulchre of Our Lord, an arm bone of St Felix the Martyr, and the jawbone of St Appolonia.

This was an age when religion played a very important part in the lives of the people, although full-size churches were spread thinly across the breadth of Bodmin Moor. Nevertheless, the moor-dwellers were not deprived of places of worship. Small chapels were built for them, scattered on the slopes of the tors in remoter areas of the moor. Roughtor boasted one and there were others at Bolventor, St Bellarmin's Tor, and Caradon Town, on the eastern fringe of the moor.

With the increase in the moorland population, a sparse network of paths now traced a pattern across the turf of the moor. In those days — as indeed now — the moorland weather might change faster than a man or beast could travel and it needed only a thin mantle of snow to disguise landmarks and cover paths and treacherous bogland alike. It was during this period that these deeply religious people put up granite crosses to mark main tracks and junctions. Since then, a great many of these tall stones have been removed, but sufficient remain to arouse the curiosity of the visitor to the moor.

A glance at the Ordnance Survey map will show them to be scattered in every corner of the moor. One of the most striking is the Longstone, commanding the approach to Minions village from the south west. Almost three metres — ten feet — tall, it is a round-topped granite pillar with a cross carved on two sides. It is described by an early nineteenth century writer as 'Standing alone on a hill of storms'. Many a weary traveller, stumbling through drifting snow, with the moorland wind roaring in his ears, must have offered up thanks for his deliverance on reaching this spot.

It was about this time that many of the villages, their populations and boundaries expanding, purchased charters from the reigning Monarch, granting them the status of towns, together with such privileges as they could afford.

Tin mining had once again assumed some importance in the twelfth century and now certain standards were set for the quality of smelted tin. King John granted the tinners — or 'stannars' — their first charter in 1201 AD. From this early document grew the great powers that the stannaries acquired in ensuing centuries. They became virtually an independent state within the county. The tinners acknowledged no master but their own Warden of the Stannaries and he, in his turn, would answer to no one but the King himself.

The stannars had their own laws, courts and prisons. They also set their own taxes. All the King asked from his Warden was that he produce tin of a high quality and ensure that a tax was levied on the amount produced and handed to the Crown. This tax on tin was the

Temple Church — once Cornwall's own Gretna Green.

main reason for allowing the tinners to go about their business without hindrance from the quarrelsome nobles. Income from this source exceeded the total amount of taxation raised in Cornwall from all other sources.

The growth of the tin trade was sufficient to make the towns of Cornwall eager for a share in its wealth and they vied with each other for the status of 'Stannary Town'. A stannary town was where the smelted tin was brought by the tinners in blocks of an agreed size. Here it would be weighed, checked for quality, and given the stannary stamp of approval. Courts of the stannary might also be held here and all such activities brought business and wealth to a town.

Liskeard and Lostwithiel eventually became the stannary towns for the miners of Bodmin Moor — indeed, Lostwithiel was the capital of Cornwall in the thirteenth century, when Edmund, grandson of King John was the Earl of Cornwall.

During Medieval times much of the British Isles was in a state of turmoil, the Kings of the land anything but secure on their throne. These royal battles for power were of little concern to Cornwall. None of the ambitious princes or peers, with their armies of retainers, held fortified castles in the county. Apart from the Church, the only great landowner was the Earl of Cornwall — and only two holders of this title ever spent any time in the county. One of these was Earl Richard, brother of Henry III. The other was Richard's son, Edmund. Edmund was the last of the Cornish Earls to actually reside in Cornwall. A deeply religious man, he died in 1299 AD leaving behind in Lostwithiel a palace, many fine old stannary buildings — and the gaol. Many of these buildings may still be seen, some incorporated in later work. The other stannary towns of this period were Helston and Truro, Penzance being added in later years.

However, the Cornish Celts were ever of an independent mind and not all the tinners marketed their metal through the stannaries. A flourishing tin-smuggling business grew in the fishing villages of Looe, Fowey and Mevagissey. It was the beginning of a way of life that was to continue unabated until the nineteenth century — and become romanticised beyond recognition in the twentieth.

A knowledge of those who farmed Bodmin Moor at this time has been gained from the excavations carried out at the Garrow Tor settlement. Here, a number of medieval 'platform' houses were built

Launceston's Castle Terrible.

on the steep slope, the living-room being dug into the hillside and a platform constructed at the other end of the house for the domestic animals. In winter, when animals and humans were kept indoors for weeks at a time by inclement weather, the smell must have been overwhelming, even for the most hardened husbandman. However, the peculiar style of construction would have solved a number of drainage problems.

This was also an age of bridge building and the ancient village of Rillaton, on the edge of the moor, lays claim to the first stone bridge in Cornwall, spanning the River Lynher. One of the most important bridges at this time was Polson Bridge, over the infant River Tamar and watched over by the great, grim fortress of Launceston Castle. This was the traditional route for the Earl of Cornwall to take when he entered the county and, in the twelfth century, the Lord of Cabilla Manor, a moorland parish, was required to meet the Earl at Polson Bridge and provide a grey cape for his use. The Earldom is now a Duchy, but the custom was recently observed when the

33

Duke of Cornwall — Charles, Prince of Wales — paid an official visit to the county.

A large part of the moor belonged to the Priory of Launceston and in 1284 a tract of land between the Rivers Fowey and Lynher was rented to twelve men for the sum of four shillings (20p) per annum. The Priory is no more and the moorland has long since reasserted its ownership, but the name, 'Twelve Mens' Moor' lives on, as do the lonely farms that bear the names of William of Trewartha and Robert Broda (or Bowda), two of the original tenants.

The Earldom of Cornwall changed hands on many occasions in the turbulent opening years of the fourteenth century, after King Edward II was cruelly murdered in a cell in Berkeley Castle and England was ruled by his widow and her lover, Roger Mortimer — the King's murderer.

In 1330, the young Edward III gained effective control of his country. Executing Mortimer, he made his brother John the Earl of Cornwall. John held the title for six years and, on his death, King Edward created the Duchy of Cornwall. His son, Prince Edward —

A typical moorland clapper bridge.

the future 'Black Prince' — then aged only seven, became the first Duke of Cornwall. Edward III also issued a charter, granting the title of Duke of Cornwall, together with all the Duchy lands, to the eldest son of the reigning monarch. This charter is followed to the present day.

It is interesting to note here, that of Edward's five sons, not one would ever sit upon the throne of England, although direct descendants of four of them were subsequently crowned.

On Bodmin Moor, the only change of note during these years was that the Knights Templar had been evicted from their hospice and it passed into the hands of the rival order of Knights Hospitallers. Their church at Temple was outside the jurisdiction of the Bishop. In later years many marriages were performed here without the participants having to observe all the formalities required by the Church. As a result it became Cornwall's own 'Gretna Green', a haven for elopers, the blessing of religious ceremony being given to many questionable marriages.

For a while all seemed set for the prosperity of Cornwall, tin mining and farming flourishing on the moor. Then, about 1348 AD bubonic plague swept into the county. The 'Black Death' raged for no more than a year or two, but during that time almost half of the population died. Crops and animals went untended with no one alive to look after them and very little tin was mined. In towns like Bodmin things were even worse and many of the newly-emptied houses quickly fell into disrepair. Happily, Cornwall escaped the peasant insurrections that broke out elsewhere in the Kingdom, as an acute shortage of labour gave the peasants an importance they had never before enjoyed. Gradually, the survivors of the Black Death began life again and the old ways were re-established.

In the middle of the century, the Black Prince crossed the moor on the way to his castle of Restormel. The whole population, sorely in need of a colourful occasion, turned out to witness the cavalcade of the Duke of Cornwall and his knights and gentlemen-at-arms.

The Prince returned to Cornwall only briefly during his remaining years. Whilst campaigning in Spain, this Warrior Prince contracted the illness from which he died in 1376 AD. King Edward III died only a year later and the throne of England was passed to Richard II, son of the Black Prince.

For the next twenty-two years, Cornwall had no Duke. King Richard remained childless and, in the last year of the century, he was murdered by his cousin who was duly acclaimed as King Henry IV.

The new King and the new century ushered in an unhappy time for Cornwall, and Cornwall's moor. Neither Henry IV, nor his successor, Henry V, had any interest in the county beyond the dues they received regularly from the stannaries — and the ships supplied by Cornish ports to transport troops to the French wars. Fewer of Bodmin Moor's great landowners resided here now. They were busy in London, scheming at the court in a bid to enlarge their Cornish estates. Others fought in France with the King's army. At Agincourt, Cornishmen fought under their own banner, Sir Henry Trelawney of Altarnon and his retainers, men of the moor, particularly distinguishing themselves.

In 1422 AD, Henry VI ascended the throne and all that had been gained in France was quickly lost during the reign of the infant King. What was even worse, the whole country was soon plunged into civil war as descendants of two of Edward III's sons, John of Gaunt and Edmund of York, fought out their rival claims to the throne.

In Cornwall, the nobility took advantage of the general confusion to settle old differences and begin new feuds. For a while, total anarchy reigned in the county, murder and open plundering going unpunished. Yet, during these desperate years, there began an upsurge in church building and renovation that would not be matched until John Wesley brought his message to Cornwall, almost 300 years later. This period of church building lasted right up until the days of the Reformation and many of the most splendid moorland churches were built at this time. Altarnon, St Neot, North Hill, Bodmin — all owe their existence to the splendid architects and clever stone masons of this era.

Then in 1483, amidst rumours of the murder of the two young sons of the late Edward IV, Richard, Duke of Gloucester, had himself crowned as King Richard III. The differences between the Cornish gentry were immediately put aside. Supporters of the rival houses of York and Lancaster joined together to oppose the child-murderer. Henry Tudor, last of the Lancastrian claimants to the throne was proclaimed King Henry VII at Bodmin.

As a centre of rebellion, Bodmin was to feature prominently in the future, but on this occasion the rebels soon realised they had been somewhat hasty. King Richard marched his army towards the West of England and the adherents of Henry Tudor felt it wise to flee the country.

THE TUDORS

However, Richard III's rule was brief. In 1485 Henry Tudor landed in England and Richard was killed at the battle of Bosworth.

Henry VII did not forget the Cornishmen who had supported his cause and fought by his side. The fortunes of many of the great families of Cornwall were founded now. Sir Richard Edgcumbe was one of the new King's firm favourites and titles and offices were showered upon him.

Another was Richard Nanfan. Given the moorland manor of Blisland and knighted by the King, Nanfan arranged the marriage between Henry's son Arthur and the infant Katherine of Aragon. Arthur died in his teens and Katherine became the wife of Arthur's brother, Henry — later Henry VIII. It can rightly be said that the consequences of this unhappy marriage changed the whole course of England's history.

Lawlessness was reluctant to release its grip on Bodmin Moor, and violence had become the accepted method of settling grievances. Gangs of outlaws roamed abroad, stealing, killing livestock and generally terrorising the countryside. Even the miners became involved. A group of tinners, disgruntled with the attempts of the Church to interfere in their affairs, attacked Bodmin Priory and put the Prior in fear of his life.

Matters came to a head in 1497 when King Henry VII levied heavy taxes on the county to pay for his war against the ever-troublesome Scots. Filled with resentment at being called upon to support a war that had nothing to do with them, the Cornish malcontents found a leader in Thomas Flamank, a vociferous Bodmin lawyer.

Flamank soon gathered 3,000 men about him at Bodmin. His numbers included the lawless elements who had been terrorising the moor for so long and there were few who were sorry to see them go as they marched across the moor to Launceston, en route to London. Their numbers grew along the way and when they reached Wells, in Somerset, they were joined by Lord Audley who took command of the rebels. Now numbering 15,000 and armed with bows and arrows and sharpened farm implements, they were a formidable force. Marching on London, they confidently expected to be joined there by the men of Kent.

They were to be bitterly disappointed. The men of Kent awaited them — but they stood in the ranks of the King's army. There was a fierce and bloody battle on Blackheath, outside London, and the ill-prepared Cornish were defeated. Many were killed and the remainder either fled or were captured.

The main body of the Cornish rebels were allowed to return to their homes, but their leaders were executed. Lord Audley, as befitted a nobleman, was beheaded. Thomas Flamank was hung, drawn and quartered on Tyburn Hill.

Henry had been generous to his rebellious Cornish subjects, but he was soon to learn that his compassion was not appreciated. Less than three months later the Cornish rose again. This time the rising was in support of Perkin Warbeck, the resourceful and plausible young man who claimed to be Richard of York, one of the two Princes murdered in the Tower of London by order of Richard III.

Once again the town of Bodmin was in the forefront of the new rebellion. It was here that Perkin Warbeck had himself proclaimed Richard IV, and again an army of Cornishmen flocked readily to his banner, encamping on the moor about Cardinham.

On this occasion some of the lesser gentry of Cornwall joined the rebels and by the time they marched on Exeter they were 6,000 strong. After a brave battle, the Cornishmen forced their way into the city, only to be beaten back again by the Earl of Devon and his men. The battle raged for twenty-four hours before the weary Cornishmen retreated, dispirited by their lack of success and the inept leadership of their adopted 'King'.

Somewhat aimlessly the army of Cornish rebels marched northwards into Somerset, but a few days later they were deserted by their leader who subsequently threw himself on the mercy of King Henry. Yet another Cornish rebellion had fizzled out. As before, Henry VII had the leaders executed and sent the rank-and-file back to Cornwall. But on this occasion the King made certain Cornwall was aware of his displeasure by fining the county heavily for its disloyalty.

For many years afterwards, while the young Prince Arthur died and his brother took both his Dukedom and his Spanish wife,

Cornwall kept her disloyal rumblings within the county.

In 1509, King Henry VIII was crowned King of England and no man could have anticipated the changes he would bring about. Henry began his turbulent reign by going to war with France. It was a habit he was to find hard to break for much of his reign. Cornishmen fought for him there, but many more remained at home, unhappy at Henry's widening rift with the Church. They were particularly incensed when the King ordered the abandonment of their 'Holy Days'. Henry was given numerous warnings about the mood of the Cornish, but he was never a man to take the advice of others.

In 1536, Henry began the process of suppressing the monasteries, beginning with the smaller establishments, such as the priory of Tywardreath. Recorded complaints against this religious house gives us an amusing picture of a ribald community led by a drunken Prior. The monks frequented taverns and were on friendly terms with women of 'suspect character'. When a Bishop visited the priory he laid down a number of rules for the monks to follow, one

Cheesewring Hill — site of an Iron Age hill fort.

being that all the windows were to be locked at night 'to prevent women coming in, or monks from leaving through them'.

The larger religious houses of Bodmin and Launceston, on either side of the moor, survived for two more years. Then they too were closed and the great tracts of land owned by them passed to the Duchy of Cornwall. For a while the moorland holdings changed tenants with great rapidity as the favourites of the unstable King took possession from those who had offended him.

Insurrection against King Henry broke out all over England, but matters were not brought to a head in Cornwall until after Henry's death, when the infant King Edward VI was on the throne, with the Duke of Somerset as his protector. In 1548, rioting broke out in Cornwall, resulting in the death of one of the new order of Churchmen. The disturbances were put down with brutal ferocity. Many men were hung, drawn and quartered on Launceston Green, the townspeople eager witnesses to the grisly spectacles.

There was worse to come. In January of 1549, Parliament passed an Act enforcing the use of an English prayer book in the churches. This order probably affected Cornwall more than any other county in the land. The people still spoke their own Cornish language. To many of the peasants who lived on the remote moor, English was a language more foreign than the familiar Latin of the Church service. The change hit at the very foundation of their lives, still very dependent upon the Church.

Yet again, Bodmin was at the hub of this new disaffection. Men marched to the town from all over the county. Bodmin Moor was well represented. With the rebels were many priests and gentry. Among their leaders was Nicholas Boyer of Bodmin, and Thomas Holmes of Blisland. Here too was Humphry Arundell of Helland, the grandson of one of the men who had terrorised Bodmin Moor in the previous century and been actively involved in the rebellion of 1497.

The Cornishmen joined forces with Devon rebels and again they marched on Exeter, the target of the earlier Cornish rebellion. This rising was put down by European mercenaries, brought in by the King. These soldiers of fortune alienated royalist and foe alike by their cruelty and a habit of slaughtering prisoners. When the rebellion collapsed, the Cornishmen limped away from Exeter, leaving behind them many of their leaders swinging on makeshift gallows in Devon.

40

But the Cornish had not yet accepted total defeat. Inexplicably, they rallied again at Sampford Courtenay, twenty miles short of the River Tamar, under the command of Humphry Arundell. A fierce battle was fought and lost here in August 1549. Arundell escaped, but only as far as Launceston. Here he was arrested by his fellow countrymen and thrown into a dungeon in the castle. Arundell was later hanged with many of his fellow conspirators and his lands given to Sir Gawen Carew, who had fought for the King.

After this last battle, Sir Anthony Kingston, the Provost Marshal, was sent into Cornwall with instructions to eliminate for ever the rebellious elements in the county. He carried out his work well. There were enough gibbet trees in Cornwall to fill a small wood. Even today many Cornishmen can point to a place in their own parish where the gallows tree once stood.

It seems that the King's Provost Marshal was not without a certain macabre sense of humour. He arrived in Bodmin to find that Nicholas Boyer, a prominent rebel, had been elected Mayor of the town. Kingston accepted the Mayor's invitation to dine but requested that, while they ate, the Mayor's men should erect a gallows for the business that was to come. After enjoying the Mayor's hospitality, Kingston, in a jovial mood, went with Boyer to inspect the finished work. The unsuspecting Mayor was persuaded to climb up to the scaffold — whereupon Kingston promptly had him hanged for a rebel. Very many more Cornishmen were hanged with less humour.

In 1553, after the death of the teenage King Edward VI, the Catholic Mary took the throne — and the reformation programme did a sharp about-turn. The clergy, who had been encouraged to marry in recent years, were now told they must put their wives from them, or be deprived of their livings. A great many chose in favour of the Church! Others — William Todd, vicar of North Hill was one — kept their wives and lost their churches.

Mary's bloody reign lasted for five years, during which time she was surrounded by plot and counter-plot and burned hundreds at the stake for the crime of heresy. Many more were executed for their opposition to her bigoted reign and in the end she alienated even her own Spanish Catholic husband. She did much to make the new Protestant religion more acceptable to her independent Cornish subjects.

Mary was followed on the throne by Elizabeth I, but even this

41

celebrated Queen proved to be vindictive when she set about restoring the Reformed Church of her father, Henry VIII. In 1577, she had Cuthbert Mayne hung by the neck in Launceston market place for preaching the Catholic faith. Before he died, he was cut down and his body hacked to pieces. His head was placed upon a pole at the castle gates. Other parts of his body went on display at Bodmin, Wadebridge and Tregony, a warning to others who might still favour the old faith.

Perhaps this execution was also to show the inhabitants of the west that their Queen had avenged the death of Agnes Prest, the foolish old woman from Northcott, only a few miles north of Launceston, who had been burned at the stake by Queen Mary.

During Queen Elizabeth's long reign, the people of Cornwall had many matters to occupy their minds. The war with Spain saw hundreds of them serving at sea with the ships of the Queen's navy, many of them captained by local men.

Men from the moor were also sent to help fight the war in Ireland. One of their leaders was Walter Raleigh, later Sir Walter Raleigh, courtier at the Queen's Court, Warden of the Stannaries, and Lord Lieutenant of Cornwall.

Bodmin Moor also shared the excitement of knowing that the great Spanish Armada had been sighted off the Cornish coast. On a July evening in 1588 the great signal beacon was lit on Caradon Hill, followed by similar beacons on Kit Hill and Dartmoor, until eventually the chain of warning bonfires stretched across all England.

The Militia, composed of tinners and peasants took up their bows and billhooks and set off for their muster points at Bodmin and Launceston, determined to resist the Spanish invasion that all men believed to be imminent. But the danger passed. Drake and his captains beat the Armada along the English Channel and the men of the moor stood down to await the next call to arms.

During Elizabeth's reign the Black Death returned to the county and Bodmin suffered greatly. The effects of the plague on the town are not surprising if Carew, the sixteenth century historian, is to be believed. He described Bodmin as a filthy and most unhealthy town where the sun never shone because of its poor siting. Nevertheless,

Fowey Valley between Bolventor and Draynes Bridge. ▶

Bodmin Moor: 'a chance to leave the cares of the world behind.'

Bodmin continued to grow in size until it was eventually able to make a bid for the title of 'County Town'.

Outside the county much of great note was taking place. Whilst Shakespeare was making his contribution to the English language, English ships carried trade goods to all corners of the world.

In Cornwall too a momentous milestone was reached. The surface tin was being used up at an ever increasing rate and in search of more, men began sinking shafts and tunnels deep into the ground. This hostile environment was one that the Cornish were to make peculiarly their own.

In 1603, James I — already King of Scotland — ascended the throne of a fragilely united Britain, and gave Cornwall its first Duke for almost sixty years. The new Duke of Cornwall, Prince Henry Stuart, discovered that many of his estates had been sold off and they were promptly ordered to be returned to the Duchy. Unfortunately, Henry did not live long enough to enjoy them. He died in 1612 and the title passed to his brother Charles. During the troubled days of his monarchy, Charles would come to know his Duchy well.

Meanwhile, the mighty navy built up by Queen Elizabeth to protect the British Isles was allowed to rot in the dockyards and the seamen of Cornwall, notorious through the years for their piratical leanings were now to suffer in their turn. From the Mediterranean came a pirate fleet more barbarous than any since the Vikings and Norsemen. With nothing to fear from Britain's navy, Turkish and Algerian ships gathered in hungry packs around the Cornish coast. Not content with the rich pickings to be taken in the English Channel, they even ventured up the rivers of Cornwall and took unfortunate Cornishmen as slaves.

It was an intolerable situation. An item in the accounts of Liskeard's Mayor for 1609/10 makes sad reading. 'Paid to J. & T. King, who had their tongues cut out and towards the ransoming of their owner and ship from the Turks . . . 2/6d (12½p).'

The few Catholics left in Cornwall made little trouble now, but a faction of the Reformed Church was making life more than a little difficult for the Establishment. These were the Puritans. They wanted to do away with all the pomp of the Church and divorce the Church itself from the State. Not unnaturally, in view of its past history, Bodmin was in the fore of such dissension. So too this time was Launceston.

In 1620, a boatload of Puritans, the 'Pilgrim Fathers' set sail from Plymouth, bound for America, a land where they hoped to be able to practise their religion unmolested by the State.

Other Puritans were less eager to cast aside their worldly possessions and seek salvation elsewhere. One, Sir Richard Robartes, bought the great tithe barn, chapel and lands of Lanhydrock. Here he built for himself the beautiful house which is among the finest in Cornwall. Sir Richard also purchased a peerage — albeit reluctantly — which made the King richer by an astounding £10,000 and gained for Sir Richard the title, Baron Robartes of Truro.

CIVIL WAR

In 1625 began the unhappy reign of King Charles I. From the beginning he was at odds with his Parliament. In order to raise money he was forced to resort to calling for 'loans'. The Vice-Warden of Cornwall's Stannaries was among those Cornishmen imprisoned for refusing to pay up. Others turned to Parliament for aid and the sides began to line up against each other, one for Parliament, the other for King. The situation worsened rapidly and by 1642 had gone too far for reconciliation. So began a Civil War, that most bitter and destructive of all conflicts.

The Cornish gentry were fairly evenly divided in their loyalties. The clergy, well aware of the profound changes that a Puritan Parliament would bring about in the Established Church, were firmly for the King. Initially the balance of power was in their hands — although a few, Charles Morton, Vicar of Blisland was one, were determinedly Puritan.

Cornwall was slow to take up any set positions within the county, but by the end of 1642, Bodmin was the King's town, while across the moor, Launceston had been occupied for Parliament.

The Cornish Royalists were cut off from outside help at first because the three nearest counties beyond her border, Devon, Dorset and Somerset, had all declared for Parliament. But the Royalists had an able general in Sir Ralph Hopton. He had earlier fled across the Tamar into Cornwall with a force of cavalry. Now, with a large army of Cornish Militia he advanced across Bodmin

Moor and took Launceston. By the beginning of October the whole of Cornwall was in the King's hands.

Hopton was reluctant to remain on the defensive, but he was unable to persuade his Cornishmen to cross the Tamar and do battle beyond their own borders. He had to wait until he had formed a force of volunteers willing to go with him. His first foray out of the county was a failure and his little army retreated across the moor to Bodmin, pursued by a Parliamentary Army which ultimately garrisoned itself at Liskeard.

On 19 January 1643, the two forces met on Braddock Down. The outcome was a resounding victory for the King's forces. Mainly Cornishmen, they fought fiercely in their own county. Their numbers were increased by the men of Liskeard, disgruntled at being forced to supply the 'foreign' Parliamentary army at their own expense and angered at seeing their church used as a stable for Parliamentary horses. The army of Parliament broke before them and were beaten all the way back to the River Tamar.

The Royalists had won an impressive victory. For many years afterwards a cannon, captured in this battle, was kept in Liskeard and fired to celebrate great happenings. One such celebration was to mark the end of the Napoleonic wars, in 1815. Unfortunately, the gun fired prematurely and cost a local man his arm. The last occasion on which it was used was in 1831, to celebrate the passing of the Parliamentary Reform Bill. Soon after this the gun was taken away to the Citadel, in Plymouth.

In April of 1642, the Royalists won another fierce battle in defence of Launceston and Hopton managed to persuade his Cornishmen to cross the Tamar in pursuit of the enemy. The excursion was short-lived. Fighting on strange soil, the Cornishmen lost their enthusiasm and Hopton had to lead them back again!

However, after fighting a number of battles well away from Bodmin Moor, the Cornish army gained sufficient confidence in its commanders to follow them to Somerset, where they became part of the Royalist army and excelled themselves in the battle for Bristol. Only half the 3,000 men survived to regret their decision, but they gained a legendary reputation for the fighting qualities of the Cornish foot-soldier.

Meanwhile, the Parliamentarians had made a surprise sortie against Bodmin, believing it to be defenceless with the main army away. However, a spirited resistance was put up by the men of

Bodmin, led by the aged Mayor of nearby Lostwithiel. The Mayor died in the fighting, but he and his men successfully beat off the Parliamentary army.

By mid-1644, the men of Cornwall had either returned to their homes, or were with the Royalist army, maintaining a desultory siege of Plymouth.

In July, the Parliamentary General, The Earl of Essex, advanced into Cornwall accompanied by Lord Robartes, the Puritan landowner whose estate of Lanhydrock had been in Royalist hands since the previous year. Essex and his army fought their way into Cornwall over the narrow Horsebridge, the battle costing 100 lives. Camping at Linkinhorne, in the shadow of the moor, Essex sent out his foragers to strip the land of animals and foodstuffs to feed his hungry army. Short of money and supplies, his army looted every house and farm they could find on Bodmin Moor.

Their actions would soon cost them very dearly.

On August 2nd, King Charles I and his nephew, Prince Maurice, mustered their troops on the rounded hill of Caradon before setting off in pursuit of Essex and his army. Afterwards the King spent a number of nights in Liskeard, lodging at the house of one of his Commissioners. The house still stands, close to the present library and a brass plaque commemorates the King's visit.

The battle between the two forces was eventually fought around Lostwithiel, the army of Parliament being forced back upon Castle Dore. Finally, abandoned by all its Generals except Major General Skippon, the army surrendered.

Stripped of its weapons, the defeated army began straggling back towards the River Tamar, crossing the moor the soldiers had pillaged only a few weeks before. The Cornish wreaked a terrible revenge. Of 6,000 Roundhead soldiers who set out from the ancient fort of Castle Dore, only 1,000 lived to reach safety. Parliament's western army was no more.

Now would have been a good time for King Charles to mount an all-out offensive against Parliament. Instead, he carried out a number of ineffective sieges and minor attacks beyond Cornwall's border and the winter passed away indecisively.

In July 1645 Parliament's troops returned on the offensive and drove the Royal army back into Cornwall. The fifteen-year old Prince Charles, Duke of Cornwall, made his headquarters at the fortified town of Launceston, while the Royalist officers did their

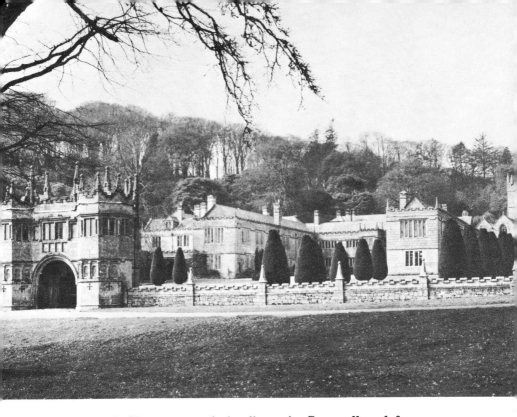

Lanhydrock House: one of the finest in Cornwall and for many years home of the Robartes family.

best to rally the county from Bodmin.

There must have been much to-and-froing across the moor by the Royalist Cavaliers, but their efforts proved in vain. The Cornish were tired of fighting and thoroughly disillusioned with the squabbling of the Royalist Generals. With their own leaders all killed in battle, there was no Cornishman of note left to rally them.

The leader of the Parliamentary army in the west was now Sir Thomas Fairfax — and he had learned from the mistakes made by Essex. Fairfax took his time advancing, preferring to woo the Cornish to his side, rather than risk facing them in battle.

When he led his troops through the villages and hamlets of Bodmin Moor in the spring of 1646 there was no looting — and little fighting. On the first day of March, Fairfax put his troops into camp at Blisland and the next day entered Bodmin without meeting any resistance. Cornwall belonged to Parliament. Only the gallant seventy-year old John Arundell, commanding the garrison of Pendennis Castle still held out against them. Not until five months later did his starving men march out of the castle with banners flying and drums beating. This was the last fortress in England to submit to Parliament.

Before long King Charles I himself was dead, beheaded on the axeman's block.

One of the first acts of the new administration was to abolish the Duchy of Cornwall. Once again the estates of the landlords were given new owners, as the victors took their spoils. Most would be restored to their original owners with the return of a King to the throne only sixteen years later, but the damage caused to many of the moorland churches had destroyed a rich heritage of church decor beyond all redemption.

Those vicars, unable to accept the new Puritanical order, were promptly dismissed. So many were removed that some churches were forced to share a minister with adjacent parishes. The responsibility for conducting weddings now passed to the civil authorities and the moor was ill-served by these officials who conducted their business from Launceston, Liskeard and Bodmin.

It was during this period that a new religious sect came to the fore on Bodmin Moor. They called themselves The Society of Friends, others called them 'Quakers'. Founded by George Fox, the Quakers went much further than the Puritans in their opposition to religious ritual in the Church, and sought to divorce the Church from the State.

In 1656, Fox was arrested and thrown into gaol at Launceston Castle. It was an experience he soon shared with many of his followers. They had a disconcerting habit of disrupting Church services by standing silently staring at the parson, and refusing to remove their hats during the service. More serious was their refusal to pay Church tithes and a number of Quakers perished in gaol for this conviction.

In 1660, the Monarchy was restored — and with it the Duchy of Cornwall. The new King, Charles II, punished his enemies but rewarded his friends generously. The stubborn old John Arundell was now dead, but his son Richard was made Lord Arundell of Trerice in recognition of the family's devotion to the King.

As things returned to normal, the pride the inhabitants of the moor had in their churches came to the fore once again. They set out to replace many of the beautiful church fittings so wantonly destroyed by Cromwell's Puritan troopers. At Altarnon church a splendid set of altar rails was built in 1684, extending the full width of the church.

A year after this, in 1685, Charles died and his brother, James II, succeeded to the throne of England. James was an avowed Catholic and for a while it seemed that another performance of religious acrobatics was to take place. There was even a rebellion, led by the Duke of Monmouth, one of Charles II's illegitimate sons. Strangely, in view of its past record, Cornwall stood back from the troubles. By 1688, the country had taken enough of James and his Papist outpourings. He was deposed and his daughter Mary, together with her husband, William of Orange, were given the throne.

There was a sigh of relief on Bodmin Moor that there were to be no changes in their churches, or their Lords of the Manors. It was no more than a sigh, men were too busy mining tin ore and working small-holdings as tenant farmers. Their years of rebellion against the English Monarchy were over. Even the language of the county was giving way to English. But Cornwall — and Bodmin Moor in particular — would always retain a character that set it apart from the land beyond the Tamar.

It was a character that did not appeal to everyone. One determined traveller who passed over the moor in 1698 was Celia Fiennes. Awed by Brown Willy, she was less attracted to the people, complaining that almost every man, woman and child smoked pipes of foul-smelling tobacco.

THE EIGHTEENTH CENTURY

At the beginning of the eighteenth century, the mines of Bodmin Moor were producing only a fraction of the tin shipped from the great mines further west. Many miners left the moor, heading westward. Those who remained gained a poor living from their diggings. But the margin between making a living and starvation was always small and miners went on the rampage more than once, demanding more money for their efforts, or a reduction in the high price of corn. Because of their immunity from all laws but their own, the tinners had an unenviable reputation for lawlessness which remained with them for very many years. Militiamen were recruited as much to contain tinners as to fight His Majesty's enemies overseas.

For the most part, independent tinners still 'streamed' for the metal they won, dependent upon water to help their efforts. For this reason they worked along the moorland rivers, especially those that flowed southwards off the moor. Traces of their ancient workings can still be seen along the Warleggan and St Neot rivers and the Witheybrook. The Cabilla workings, near Warleggan village, were worked extensively for centuries.

These streamworkings provided enough ore to keep smelting houses busy at St Neot and Linkinhorne, but more than tin was being worked now. Copper was being brought out of the Wheal Mary — then known as Pouldiste Copper Mine — south of St Neot. There was also a considerable amount of silver ore in the same mine. To the south east, where the River Fowey flows through the beautiful Glynn valley, small quantities of gold were discovered, a heavy signet ring being made from it for a member of the Glynn family. There is also an old working, known locally as 'the gold-diggings', on the moor close to Minions village.

Much slate was also quarried around the edge of the moor. Off the moor to the north, beyond Camelford is the great quarry of Delabole. A mile in circumference, it is deep enough to comfortably bury St Paul's Cathedral. There are also a number of slate quarries near St Neot, together with huge underground caverns where slate has been dug from the hillsides.

But there was more than heavy industry here. Sheep grazed on the high moor and women in remote cottages and farms spun wool and weaved cloth for the Bodmin tailor who advertised a full suit of warm clothing for 3/- (15p).

There were skilled craftsmen too. John Arnold of Bodmin learned the trade of watchmaking from his father and then went to London where he found both fame and fortune. In 1764 he made a watch that was claimed to be the smallest ever. Set in a ring, it was given to George III as a birthday present.

**Cheesewring above the quarry —
occasionally used by trainee mountaineers. ▶**

Daniel Gumb was a man who never achieved national fame, but was well known on Bodmin Moor in the early eighteenth century. Born in Linkinhorne parish, he learned the trade of a stonecutter. But his inclinations were towards philosophy, mathematics and astronomy. When he married, he moved to the slopes of Stowe's Hill, below the Cheesewring — a very lonely place in those days. Here he built himself an unusual rock shelter and pursued his studies. The remains of the unusual 'house' where he and his wife raised a large family may still be seen close to the Cheesewring quarry. On the stone that formed the roof is carved a geometrical diagram, and his name and the date, 1735, is carved on a nearby rock. His work may still be seen on a headstone in Linkinhorne churchyard.

At dusk, on an August day in 1743, four mounted men were lost on Bodmin Moor and seemed destined to spend the night on its windy wastes until the bells of Bodmin guided them off the moor to safety. The leader of the party was The Reverend John Wesley. It was the first visit to the moor by the man who was to influence the lives of Cornishmen more than any other in Cornwall's long history.

For forty-six years Wesley crossed and re-crossed the moor on his thirty one visits. By the time of his death in 1791, 'preaching houses' or chapels, had sprung up in almost every moorland hamlet. Wesley's 'Methodism' had a following that rivalled that of the Established Church. His success had been hard-won, his early mission aimed at the souls of the miners. They were notoriously violent men and Wesley faced their violence on more than one occasion. In the end he won them over and they became the backbone of his movement in Cornwall.

At Trewint, near Altarnon, Digory Isbell and his wife Elizabeth built a two-roomed extension to their small cottage for Wesley and his fellow preachers. From here, in 1744, Digory set out without complaint to guide John Wesley across a moor rendered almost featureless by a snowstorm, the whereabouts of the narrow path discernible only to a man of the moor.

Another man who would have been familiar with Bodmin Moor was William Bligh, whose family home was at Tinten manor, close to St Tudy. There is some doubt as to whether he was actually born

◀ **Inspecting the Pythagoras theorem carving by Daniel Gumb over his cave near Minions.**

here, but he would often have visited his grandfather from Plymouth, where William's father was a Customs official. William Bligh's name is synonymous with the mutiny on HMS *Bounty*, but the whole of Bligh's life involved adventure and controversy.

William Bligh was already an experienced sailor when he accompanied Captain Cook on his third voyage around the world, the voyage on which Cook was murdered by the natives of the Hawaiian Islands. Then, in 1789, as Lieutenant Bligh, in command of HMS *Bounty*, he was cast adrift with eighteen of his crew in an open boat only twenty-three feet long. In this craft, without the aid of a chart, he sailed across 4,000 miles of ocean to Timor, in the East Indies.

At this stage, most people would have considered they had experienced adventure enough for a lifetime. Not so William Bligh. At the famous Battle of Copenhagen, in 1801, we find him in command of HMS *Glatton,* part of Nelson's fleet. Four years later he arrived in Australia as Governor of New South Wales. It was a turbulent governorship and in 1808 he was deposed by the army and held in prison until 1810 when he was shipped back to England.

Incredibly, this dramatic incident failed to put an end to Bligh's long and fascinating career. A year after his return to England he was promoted to the rank of Rear Admiral. Three years later, at the age of 61, he was made Vice Admiral of the Blue. This remarkable man died in 1814 and is buried at Lambeth, London.

Long before the death of Admiral Bligh, the roads of Cornwall — so long regarded as a disgrace by all who had to travel them, had been greatly improved. The isolation so long enjoyed by the county was coming to an end. In 1789 we have the first mention of the Jamaica Inn at Bolventor, serving the new turnpike road cut through the heart of Bodmin Moor to link Launceston and Bodmin. With the improved roads to the heart of Cornwall, Launceston lost its status. In 1780 a new gaol was completed at Bodmin to take the place of Launceston's crumbling 'Castle Terrible'. Now the town behind so many acts of rebellion was well on its way to take the coveted title of 'County Town'.

Before the century drew to a close, Louis XVI and Marie

The cottage at Trewint used by Wesley on his many visits to Cornwall. ▶

Antoinette had kneeled before the guillotine in France, Napoleon Bonaparte had taken the reins of government — and Britain and France were at war again. For Cornwall and its moor, the war removed the threat of starvation from thousands of desperate tinners. They joined the army of Sir Arthur Wellesley — later to become the Duke of Wellington — in the campaigns that would culminate in the Battle of Waterloo. At Waterloo and the lesser known fight at Quatre Bras, only forty-eight hours before, the Cornwall Regiment suffered 570 casualties, half their total strength.

Back at home the Cornwall Militia were kept busy performing guard duty at Dartmoor Prison. Other French prisoners-of-war, having given a pledge to be on good behaviour roamed the streets of Bodmin Town unmolested.

The heroes of Waterloo returned to find that the mines of Cornwall had undergone a dramatic change. Now they extended deep underground, with engines to pump out the water and raise ore to the surface.

For the non-mining ex-soldier there were dubious bargains to be had in the market places around the moor. In Camelford an unappreciated wife was auctioned to an eager purchaser for 2/6d (12½p). An ex-soldier secured an even greater bargain at Bodmin market. His secondhand wife cost him a mere sixpenny piece (2½p) — and the halter with which her husband had led her to market was thrown in free!

Politics had now become a serious matter to a great many men and the movement for parliamentary reform was gaining momentum. A petition to the High Sheriff demanding changes bore the signatures of many of the county's wealthiest men. A look at the newspapers of the day provide some of the reasons for their concern.

Two MPs were returned for Camelford and control of the town's votes was keenly contested. In December, 1822, the Riot Act was read during a dispute over possession of a house between followers of two sponsors. In October 1823 the dispute took a novel turn. One of the sponsors erected a house in Camelford to house prospective voters. His rival, the Earl of Darlington, immediately claimed mineral rights over the land, had a mine dug beneath the new house and set charges. Watched by many interested spectators, the fuse was lit — and the house tumbled to the ground!

It is small wonder that the government of the day bowed to public pressure in 1832 and reduced the number of parliamentary seats in Cornwall from 42 to 10. Two seats had already been taken away from Grampound in 1821, when it was disclosed that Sir Manasseh Lopes had paid each of the forty eligible voters £50 each to vote for him — with an additional bonus for the Mayor. Grampound was by no means the smallest of the boroughs. For some time the two MPs for the tiny borough of Bossiney were sent to London by a single vote.

Another much needed reform was carried out in the 1820s by Sir Robert Peel when he amended the Penal Code. It was long overdue. Prior to this the Criminal Law covered a tangled mass of crimes, many of them petty, for which death was the only penalty. Matters were so bad that for many years juries refused to convict even guilty offenders because the crime did not merit the punishment it would bring. Such consideration had not saved the entire male population of Temple a few years earlier. The men — two of them — were both hanged for sheep stealing.

MINING

In 1837, a discovery was made at Caradon which was to change the whole character and the landscape of the eastern moor. James Clymo, a shrewd mine captain, working with his two sons, discovered rich copper ore deep in the rounded hill of Caradon, where King Charles I had once mustered the Royalist army, on his way to a victorious battle. The ore was so rich and plentiful that within a few years more than twenty mines crowded the moor around Caradon. Engine house chimneys belched smoke from the heights of Caradon, Stowe's Hill, Sharptor, Darley Tor and Craddock Moor and, in between, the valleys echoed to the clatter of stamps and the rumble of ore trucks.

Hopeful latecomers swarmed over the surrounding countryside, pockmarking the moorland in their search for more of the rich ore.

The discovery coincided with a falling off in the world-wide demand for tin. Miners from the west of Cornwall swarmed to the moor in their thousands. It was the beginning of such moorland villages as Crow's Nest, Darite and Minions, while established villages, including St Cleer, increased their population by as much

as five hundred percent.

For many years the moorland mines provided a preview of the mining camps that were to spring up in America many years later. Shanty towns were thrown up all over the moor with gin houses and brothels to take back the miners' hard-earned pay. Stories are authenticated of men spending several days and nights on a single spree in these establishments — and of irate wives arriving to drag them home. In nearby Liskeard no decent woman dared to go outside her house after dark on settling day.

But it was not only the miners who displayed such a lack of inhibitions and zest for life on Bodmin Moor. In 1844 a 'Temperance' meeting was held on Roughtor and attended by an estimated 10,000 revellers. It rapidly degenerated into drunken dancing and singing that lasted through the night.

Before long a railway line was brought up to the eastern moor, extending on granite sleepers around the slope of Stowe's Hill to Kilmar Tor, with branches dropping to the bottom of the Phoenix Valley, torn-up by the copper mines sited there. The railway line linked the mines with the Moorswater-Looe Canal. From the high moor the trucks ran down to Moorswater, using gravity and the weight of their loads. During the early years the trucks, laden with coal, were pulled back to the mines by horses, but by 1862 the canal had given way to an extension of the railway line and a little saddle-tank engine named *Caradon* pulled the ore trains. It was joined within a few years by *Cheesewring* and *Kilmar*.

These were not the first railway engines seen in the vicinity of the moor. As early as 1834, a line was opened to follow the course of the Camel River upstream from Wadebridge as far as Wensford. It was influential in opening up many mines around Blisland, St Breward and Roughtor.

A spur from this line ran to Bodmin and was opened in time for a special excursion to be arranged on 13 April, 1840, to view the public execution outside Bodmin Gaol of the brothers William and James Lightfoot, convicted of murder. The crowds returned again in August 1844, when the jealous young cripple, Matthew Weeks, was hanged for the murder of his eighteen year-old sweetheart,

◀ Caradon Hill: site of the great
copper discoveries in the nineteenth century.

Charlotte Dymond, on Roughtor.

This murder aroused the anger of the Cornish populace, but it is a tragic tale. Matthew Weeks and Charlotte Dymond lived and worked at the lonely Penhale farmhouse and, on their walks together over the moors, Charlotte would tease the jealous young cripple with stories of imaginary sweethearts with whom she had flirted.

She did it once too often.

On Sunday 4 April, 1844, the young couple went for a walk across the moor towards Roughtor — but neither returned. Two days later Charlotte's body was discovered in an old stream bed near Roughtor Ford. Her throat had been cut from ear to ear. Weeks was swiftly apprehended and 20,000 people watched him pay with his own life for his crime.

Right: Gateway of Bodmin Prison, where 20,000 people watched the hanging of Matthew Weeks.
Below: Engine used on one of the country's earliest lines in the Camel Valley.

A monument was erected at the spot where Charlotte Dymond's body was found and she is said to haunt Roughtor to this day.

Charlotte's ghost is not the only one to haunt Bodmin Moor. The most famous is undoubtedly that of John Tregeagle. In life reputed to be a cruel and unjust man, he was steward to Lord Robartes of Lanhydrock. It was said he had a pact with the Devil and for his sins his spirit is doomed to bale out Dozmary Pool with a holed limpet shell, tormented by demons. When the torment becomes unbearable, Tregeagle's ghost runs howling across the moor on stormy nights, heading for the sanctuary of the Roche Rock chapel.

This is just one of the many legends surrounding John Tregeagle. It is perhaps surprising that the moor, occupied for thousands of years by primitive man and superstitious miner, does not have many more ghosts. The miners certainly believed in such beings. They heard them often, underground, mining their own invisible lodes. Many unexplained sounds have been heard even in this century. In a shaft known as 'Roaring Shaft', on the Wheal Friendship Mine on Goonzion Down, miners reported hearing a noise 'like a battery of stamps falling regularly with thuds that reverberated through the ground'. This was the same sound heard by miners who worked in the shaft a hundred years before.

Many a miner, working deep underground, would break off a piece of his pasty and leave it for the 'little men' before he finished his own meal — and no underground miner would begin Christmas unless he had left something behind for his unseen companions to eat over the holiday.

By the middle of the nineteenth century John Wesley's followers had gained ascendency over the new generation of miners and permanent houses and chapels took the place of shanty hut and gin-parlour. Most people breathed a sigh of relief at the change, others grumbled that John Wesley's brand of sober religion had taken much of the fun from the lives of the easy-going miner.

It cannot be disputed that the Cornish miner had need of some frivolity in his life. The search for copper took him deep under the earth. At the beginning and end of an exhausting shift, many miners had to climb a thousand feet of ladders. Lungs that had been

Monument to Charlotte Dymond on the marshes
below Roughtor where she was murdered in 1844.

labouring in extreme heat for hours would suddenly suck in the fresh, frosty air of a winter morning. Numbed and tired fingers fumbled the ladder rungs, and falls were a daily occurrence. Gunpowder also claimed its share of victims and at the height of the mining boom, the average age of those buried at St Cleer was no more than twenty-one years.

It could be truly said that for every man made rich by mining, at least a hundred more went to a premature death. For almost every one of these young miners, the only memorial is an engine-house, standing roofless, windowless and neglected over the mines where so many men died.

But the incredible copper boom was not to last. There were perhaps thirty great years, thirty struggling years — and then it was all over. Foreign mines — in many cases developed with the help of Cornish expertise — had brought cheaper copper on to the market.

During the mining heyday, nature flexed its own muscles on the moor. In 1847 there was a tremendous 'cloudburst' in the vicinity of Davidstow and two rivers of usually modest proportions roared from the moor, sweeping aside houses and bridges. The rivers were the Inny and the Camel, one flowing south eastwards to the Tamar, the other south and west to the sea. For many years afterwards, people in the valleys could point to debris, lodged twenty feet up in the trees, as a reminder of the great flood.

With the decline of the mines, great inroads were made into the moor by farmers who reclaimed hundreds of acres of land, clearing away gorse and fern and enclosing their newly-won pastures.

When world-wide demand increased for china clay, formed by nature from decomposed granite, it seemed for a while that the granite uplands of Bodmin Moor had found a substitute for the tin and copper it had produced for thousands of years. China clay *is* mined here, but its quality has failed to match that of the area north of St Austell, where man's ingenuity has sculpted a whole new landscape.

Neither did quarrying prove to be a venture to replace mining. The great hole in Stowe's Hill is ample proof that much granite was

'Roofless engine house: the only memorial for the many miners who met an early death.' ▶

Bearah Tor where craftsmen still cut and polish granite.

taken from the moor, but of the early quarries only three remain. The two largest are in the Delank valley. The other is the beautifully sited Bearah Tor Quarry on the eastern moor, where craftsmen still cut and polish granite for despatch to all parts of the world.

The Phoenix Mine claimed the unusual distinction of having had Naval divers working underground. In 1883 they were employed to carry out essential work on a flooded shaft, 200 fathoms below ground. Despite this, the mine managed only to limp along until it was closed down, after years of operating at a loss, in 1894.

The Wheal Phoenix was opened up again in the twentieth century and the Prince of Wales shaft named after a visit by the future King George V. This visit is remembered still by a number of local people, but the venture was doomed to an early failure. After reaching a depth of 200 fathoms this shaft was abandoned in 1914, and the mine closed. It has given to Cornwall one of the most impressive engine houses to be seen anywhere in the county.

THE MOOR TODAY

The twentieth century has undoubtedly brought about as many changes as any other period of Bodmin Moor's long history. Due to modern technology and the advent of the selective weedkiller, the moor has shrunk faster than ever before. Crops, conifers and pasture are taking the place of marshland and lush fern slope.

There is not a village that does not have its crop of pebble-dash bungalows. Some — Pensilva, Tremar, Commonmoor and St Cleer are but a few — have undergone brutal changes of character. The accent of England-across-the-Tamar is heard more often than the broad and distinctive accent of the true Cornishman, once quite unintelligible to the first-time visitor.

The railway lines to the moorland mines have gone, the bridges torn down to allow free passage along the narrow roads for American tank-transporters and ammunition lorries, preparing for

Trenant Chapel — agricultural machinery is now stored where worshippers once knelt in prayer.

the D-Day landings in France.

The chapels, once milestones of man's faith and enthusiasm, are struggling for their very existence. A few have already conceded defeat. One wonders what Petherick Higman, John Crispin and Thomas Polkinhorne would have thought about the retreat of their religion. They lie in the neglected little burial ground at Trenant, where a small stream flows beneath a delightfully narrow clapper bridge on the Draynes-St Neot road. Nearby is a caravan site and, closer still, agricultural machinery is garaged in the chapel that bears forlorn witness to the fact that it was built in 1826 and hopefully restored in 1883.

Sacrifices to the needs of war are inevitable, but on Bodmin Moor is a memorial of far greater value to the sons and daughters of Cornwall's fallen warriors than a plaque on a damp church wall. The beautiful area of Roughtor was given to the nation in memory of those who lost their lives whilst serving with the 43rd (Wessex)

Jamaica Inn at Bolventor known to tourists from all over the world.

Division in the North West European campaign, 1944-5. A plaque commemorating this stands in the remains of the medieval chapel on the tor. No man could wish for a finer memorial.

Only three miles from Roughtor is the complex of runways and taxiways of Davidstow airfield. Built by the Americans, it was quickly abandoned, their plans foiled by the persistent moorland mists. One of their aircraft crash-landed on Langstone Downs, beyond lonely Wardbrook Farm. One of the survivors staggered to the farm only to learn that the two women occupants did not open the door to *anyone* after dark. The unfortunate American airman had to continue along the track to Henwood village before he was able to obtain assistance.

Moorland mist has affected the plans of many men and women over the centuries, but none has put the temporary set-back to such enduring advantage as the authoress, Daphne du Maurier. Lost on the moor, one wet, misty November evening many years ago, she drew upon the experience to write *Jamaica Inn.* Her novel brings travellers to Bolventor from all over the world to see the now famous inn.

There is much on the moor for the visitor. History, incredible beauty, peace — and a chance to leave the cares of the world behind. Parts of the moor are fenced off and some put down to afforestation, but the moor has much to offer the walker who travels with an Ordnance Survey map — and a sense of responsibility.

I have walked for very many miles over Bodmin Moor and seen it in all its varied moods. It remains for me what it has always been. One of the most beautiful places in this scenic county. Perhaps, if the moor enchants future generations of visitors and residents, their combined voices will ensure that it never disappears entirely in the ill-named guise of 'progress'.

Moorland Towns and Villages

ALTARNUN

This is a most pleasing little village, tucked far enough away from the main A30 road across the moor to have retained much of its character. The 'Penponta' of the Domesday Book, the village was named for St Non — or Nonna — whose altar was probably preserved here. Many Dark Age Saints possessed portable stone altars which they carried with them wherever they went.

St Non was the mother of St David, patron Saint of Wales, and she came here early in the sixth century. Her holy well, now in a state of disrepair was once believed to cure insanity. After being immersed in its waters until semi-conscious any unfortunate creature would have been less inclined to violence, but it is doubtful whether such a dowsing had a lasting effect!

The beautiful church, known as 'The Cathedral of the Moor', dates from the fifteenth century, although there are traces of the earlier Norman building. The Celtic cross in the churchyard is a reminder of the church that St Non built here in the sixth century.

Nevil Northey Burnard, a brilliant sculptor, was born here in 1818 and carved many local works before going to London to find fame — and unhappiness. His is a tragic story. At the peak of his career he dined with the Queen, made a marble bust of the infant Edward, Prince of Wales, and was feted in London society. Then Burnard's much-loved daughter, Lottie, died. The loss affected Burnard so deeply that he gave up everything and returned to his own county as a vagrant, dying a pauper's death in Redruth workhouse in 1878.

One of Burnard's works is a carving of the head of John Wesley, over the door of the chapel in Altarnun. He also carved two of the headstones in Altarnun churchyard.

Carving of John Wesley by Burnard at Altarnun. ▶

BLISLAND

Unless one approaches the village from the east it is difficult to appreciate that this is a moorland village. Indeed, it is not typical of a Cornish community, being set around a village green — complete with friendly village 'pub'. Until recently the green could boast a collection of beautifully mature trees. Unfortunately, time and disease have taken their toll and now only the stumps remain. It is pleasing to see, however, that the villagers have wasted no time in replacing them with new trees to benefit future generations.

The church, with its unusual dedication to Saints Protus and Hyacinth, is Norman, with additions being added in most centuries since. The Norman font was discovered in the churchyard in 1868 and restored early in the present century.

There are a number of interesting old houses in and around the village and the manor of Blisland was held by King Harold before the Norman Conquest.

The victorious Parliamentary Army, led by Lord Fairfax, camped here on 1 March 1646, on its way to subjugate the whole of Cornwall.

BODMIN

This is the town from which the moor receives its name, although Bodmin actually lies off the south western edge of the moor. The moor was once known by the much more appropriate name of 'Foweymoor'.

Bodmin lies more or less in the centre of Cornwall and has always regarded itself as the county's premier town. This is a very ancient community — some historians claim there was a temple here, dedicated to the God Apollo, a thousand years before Christianity was born. Later, an important priory was sited here and among his 'priviliges' the Prior could claim a market, a fair, a pillory — and a gallows!

The church has been called the largest, tallest and fairest of all Cornish churches — but this observation was made before the spire fell in 1699. Inside the church can be seen the ivory casket that once held the bones of St Petroc who founded a priory here in the sixth century. Early historians assert that in the year 905 AD King Edward the Elder obtained a decree from the Pope and settled a Bishop's See here. Later historians dispute this, insisting that there was not a Bishop of Cornwall until Edward's son, Athelstan, gave Bishop Conan a cathedral at St Germans in 926 AD.

During the Middle Ages, Bodmin was the centre of the county's unrest against the Crown, and on three occasions a rebel army set off from here to fight against the King of England.

Not surprisingly, Bodmin and the immediate vicinity has produced some distinguished fighting-men. The obelisk dominating the skyline above the town commemorates Sir Walter Raleigh Gilbert. A Lieutenant General in the Indian Army, the Sikhs surrendered to him after the Punjab campaign of 1848-9. One result of this campaign was the acquisition of the famous Kohinoor Diamond which was presented to Queen Victoria and now forms part of the Crown Jewels. It is appropriate that the Crown Jewels should have been brought to Bodmin Gaol for safe-keeping during the 1914-18 war.

Another General was Lord Vivian of Glynn House, a couple of miles away, overlooking the Fowey River. Lord Vivian commanded the sixth Cavalry Brigade of the German Legion at the Battle of Waterloo. Glynn House is now owned by Dr Peter Mitchell who in 1978 won the Nobel Prize for Chemistry for the work he carried out here.

Closer to Bodmin than Glynn House, is Lanhydrock. For long the home of the Robartes family, it is now owned by the National Trust. A magnificent house with beautiful gardens, it is well worth a visit.

BOLVENTOR

Truly a moorland village, Bolventor is situated in the very heart of the moor on the A30 road. Here is the Jamaica Inn, made famous by Daphne du Maurier's novel. Originally 'The New Inn', serving the turnpike road across the moor, it was renamed in honour of a member of the local land-owning Rodd family, on his return from a high Government post in Jamaica.

It was one of this family, resident at Trebartha, across the moor, who built the tiny church. Almost unnoticed behind a busy lay-by, its walls green with mould and the churchyard overgrown and neglected, this little church has an apologetic air, but its register truly reflects the hard life of Bodmin Moor in the middle of the nineteenth century. The first baptism is of Fanny, daughter of the toll-gate keeper at Palmers Bridge. The first marriage is of a tin-streamer and both he and his young bride scratched out an 'X' in place of a signature. But perhaps the burials reveal more than anything else the harsh environment of the moor. Most are babies whose frail constitutions could not withstand the damp and raw cold of a lonely moorland hut.

Bolventor is reputed to have its own ghost, that of a sailor who was murdered before he had finished his drink at the Jamaica Inn.

Opposite the inn is the narrow road to St Neot that passes Dozmary Pool, the thirty-acre moorland 'lake', where another ghost,

**Bolventor Church: 'almost unnoticed
behind a lay-by, its register reflects the hard life of the Moor.'**

that of John Tregeagle, does penance for the sins he committed during his lifetime, his voice carried on the wind that howls about the tors. Somewhere in this same Pool lies *Excalibur*, King Arthur's mighty sword, while on its shores have been found the tiny, stone implements of early man.

At the edge of Dozmary Pool a typical moorland farmhouse is hunkered down in silent disapproval of wind, weather, Tregeagle's ghost — and summer visitors.

CAMELFORD

The name of this small town is derived from the river, which was formerly known as the 'Alan'. Camalan is 'Crooked River' and this town grew up about the Camalan Ford. Because of its proximity to Roughtor and the high rainfall area of the moor, Camelford probably has more rain than any other Cornish town.

Camelford lays tenuous claim to being King Arthur's Camelot, with Slaughter Bridge, a mile upstream, the scene of his last battle. Less romantic historians declare that the battle was more likely to have been fought between the Saxons and a combined army of Cornish and Danes in the year 823 AD. A Dark Age stone close to the site — known as King Arthur's Tomb — throws little light on either alternative. The Latin inscription on the stone reads, *Latini ic iacit filius Macari*, or, 'Latinus lies here the son of Macarus'. The name is repeated in Ogham script — of Irish origin.

Camelford has found little favour with either chroniclers or travellers through the ages. Leland refers to it as 'a poore village', and that inveterate traveller, Celia Fiennes, dismissed its accommodation as being 'indifferent'.

Disgruntled husbands found its market place more to their liking. During the Napoleonic wars of the early nineteenth century a wife was sold here for 2/6d (12½p).

Parliamentary rivalry was excessively keen in the nineteenth century and the story has already been told of the lengths to which Camelford's parliamentary patrons were prepared to go to ensure the success of their candidates.

Nowadays, Camelford is a rather pretty town, with only the growl of summer traffic to disturb its narrow streets.

CARDINHAM

The name is supposed to mean 'The Rock-man's Home' and there are enough rocky tors north east of the village to make such an interpretation acceptable. Perhaps the 'Rock-man' was St Bellarmin, whose chapel and holy well were once here.

A Norman Castle once stood south of Cardinham. Built soon after the Conquest by Robert Fitzturold, the first Lord of Cardinham, it stood for 300 years, not far from an earlier Iron Age enclosure. There is little to be seen of the castle now but its outline.

In the side of a deep, wooded valley south west of Cardinham is a lead mine that was worked in the nineteenth century and found to be rich in silver. There were many other lead mines in the area, some being worked until the beginning of this century.

This little known village boasts a fine fifteenth century church in which is a brass commemorating Thomas Awmarle, a Rector of the parish in the fourteenth century and there is an early cross in the churchyard.

DAVIDSTOW

A bleak, scattered parish, almost a thousand feet high on the northern edge of the moor. There is little here but a fifteenth century church and a few houses.

Charlotte Dymond, the eighteen-year-old servant girl murdered on Roughtor in 1844, lived here in a lonely farmhouse, and she is buried in Davidstow churchyard, surrounded by the graves of the family for whom she and her murderer worked.

Close by are the pot-holed runways and derelict buildings of the World War II bomber base built here by the Americans in 1942. At such a height, low cloud and persistent mist made landing a hazardous business for the pilot of a heavy bomber, exhausted after hours of flying over German-occupied Europe.

HENWOOD

Tucked away in a small valley, in the shadow of Sharptor and the historic Twelve Men's Moor, Henwood has not escaped the attentions of modern architects, but it remains one of the prettiest of moorland villages.

There is no church here, Henwood being part of Linkinhorne parish. But there is a chapel, almost 150 years-old and now, sadly, attended by no more than half-a-dozen ageing worshippers.

This village was here long before extensive mining was undertaken in the area and the family bearing the name of Henwood still live in the parish and are able to trace their ancestry back for hundreds of years.

On the skyline to the south of the village is the ruin of the Prince of Wales shaft engine house, one of the most attractive in Cornwall. The mine, part of the great Phoenix United, closed in 1914, but tin was mined here in the seventeenth century and tin streaming carried out along the Witheybrook for centuries before this.

LAUNCESTON

Not truly a moorland town, Launceston and its priory have had such an influence on Bodmin Moor that no history would be complete without mentioning this most ancient town.

The town is dominated by the ruins of the castle — once known as 'Castle Terrible', built here to guard the important river crossing. Robert of Mortain had the stone castle built on the site of an earlier wooden fortress. The green inside the southwest gateway was the scene of many executions until 1821 and visitors who leave through the northeast gateway pass the dungeon where George Fox, father of the Quakers, was imprisoned in 1656.

Launceston was once a walled town and the road still passes beneath the south gateway. Alongside the churchyard of St Thomas's fifteenth century church is the site of the twelfth century Augustinian Priory, victim of the Reformation. Opposite, is a fascinating little fifteenth century pack-horse bridge, spanning the River Kensey beside a ford. Beyond the river and up the hill is the Catholic church with a shrine dedicated to Cuthbert Mayne, martyred in Launceston in 1577.

In 1540, when the privilege of sanctuary was withdrawn from many places, Launceston was allowed to retain this ancient custom.

All criminals, except those guilty of murder, rape, highway robbery, burglary or sacrilege, could find a sanctuary for life here. This privilege was kept until the reign of James I.

Launceston has a very interesting little museum housed in a fine Georgian building.

LISKEARD

Again, this is not really a moorland town, but, for travellers by rail, Liskeard station lies closer to the moor than any other. A thriving little market town, life has become much more relaxed since the by-pass took through-traffic from its narrow streets.

According to the historian Fortescue Hitchins, tradition has a Roman Legion camped here, but proof is as hard to find as are traces of the ancient castle that was one of the Cornish palaces of the Duke of Cornwall, with a park and two hundred deer.

Certainly, Liskeard is very ancient and as a stannary town was of some importance in the Middle Ages. It was also famous for its leather-work, supplying boots and shoes to most of Cornwall.

Liskeard saw the armies of both King and Parliament as they passed through here in victory and in defeat. They would have cost the town more dearly than the 700 soldiers who arrived here in 1624 and were given 4/- (20p) by the Mayor, for 'bread and beer'. In the same year the Mayor paid out 2/- for a man to erect a gallows, with an additional 1/10d for the wood. Perhaps the most intriguing entry in the Mayoral accounts for 1650, says simply, 'For whipping Alice Piper — 6d'. One wonders what offence poor Alice had committed to incur the Mayor's displeasure?

MINIONS

Minions lays claim to being the highest village in Cornwall, with the highest inn — at more than 1,000 feet (304 metres). The unusual

◀Fifteenth century packhorse bridge at Launceston spanning River Kensey.

name for this village is said to originate in Minions mound, a huge mass of earth at the west end of the village, purported to be the grave of King Minion, a Celtic 'King', of whom nothing is known but his name.

Minions is increasing in popularity with summer visitors because of the great number of interesting features in the immediate area — in addition to its situation, surrounded by moorland on all sides.

At the edge of the village are The Hurlers, Bronze Age stone circles dating from 1,500 BC. Here too is the barrow from which the Rillaton Cup was taken in the last century. A few hundred yards away is the 'Longstone', standing alone on the moor. The crosses incised on either side of the Longstone were most probably carved in the Middle Ages, although one school of thought would date them from the Saintly period of the Dark Ages.

Across the moor from the village is the now deserted granite quarry on Stowe's Hill, its granite cliff rising to the Cheesewring, a well-known group of balancing rocks. Beyond the Cheesewring — so named from its similarity to the shape left by a cloth-enclosed cheese when the whey has been wrung from it — is an Iron Age hill fort.

All around the village are ruined engine houses and wired-off mine shafts, reminders that this village was at the heart of the copper boom of the 1830s. From Minions it is possible to follow the granite sleepers of the old mineral railway around Stowe's Hill and onto the lonely wastes of the heart of the moor.

NORTH HILL

One of the most important of the moorland villages, with a church to match its status. It is interesting to take a walk around the churchyard and see how the houses of the village huddle close about the church.

Inside the fourteenth-fifteenth century church are a number of fine monuments to the Spoure family who occupied nearby Trebartha Manor for almost 250 years. The manor had a very

Stone formation near Minions. ▶

romantic history. Occupying a beautiful moorland valley, the original manor house was given to one of William the Conqueror's Normans, who took the name of Trebartha for his own. Here, in this picturesque and tranquil setting, the Trebartha line continued unbroken until 1497. There being no male heir, the young Anne Trebartha took the property in marriage to Thomas Spoure, a Captain in Henry VII's army, sent to Cornwall to put down the rising led by Perkin Warbeck. The Spoure line continued until Henry Spoure died in 1687, at the age of ten years. His sister Mary inherited the property and survived two husbands, but her own infant son died before he could inherit Trebartha. When Mary died in 1729 she willed the house and estate to her cousin, Captain Francis Rodd, to whom she was then engaged.

Thus, from the time Trebartha was taken by conquest in 1066, until it was purchased for the wood of its trees in 1940, Trebartha passed in succession through different branches of the one family. The last manor house was pulled down in 1948, ending almost 900 years of a settled way of life that has left a lasting mark on this most beautiful and tranquil of Cornish valleys.

ST BREWARD

Described by historian Fortescue Hitchins as 'An extensive but sterile parish', St Breward is named after a warlike thirteenth century Bishop of Exeter who fought against infidels in Palestine. The village was once known as Simonward — and Simon Ward, we are told, was brewer to King Arthur's household!

The two highest tors on the moor are in this parish, Brown Willy 1377 feet (420 metres) and Roughtor 1311 feet (400 metres). The church of St Breward also claims to be sited higher than any other church in the county. Dating from the fifteenth century, it incorporates much of the earlier Norman building, but little of the interior escaped the attentions of J.P. St Aubyn, whose method of church restoration was, as often as not, to tear everything out and 'begin again'.

Holy well at St Cleer. ▶

ST CLEER

One of the moorland villages whose population increased so dramatically when copper was discovered at nearby Caradon Hill. It was the centre of a parish of rough, tough miners until they came under the sobering influence of Methodism. There is still a large Methodist chapel here, but others are now dwelling-houses.

The village boasts an attractive fifteenth century church with a number of Norman features and a fine tower. Further along the road towards Tremar is a sensitively restored holy well.

St Cleer is one of those moorland villages whose character is being rapidly swamped by modern housing projects that will soon take in Tremar and reach out towards Darite and Crow's Nest.

The stone tomb of Trethevy Quoit is nearby and King Doniert's Stone is in the same parish, on the road to Redgate. Only a short distance from King Doniert's Stone is Golitha Falls, where the river Fowey tumbles down a rocky course, through a high-sided, wooded valley that is a popular beauty spot.

ST NEOT

One of the most ancient and well-known of moorland villages, St. Neot is tucked away in an attractive valley on the southern edge of the moor.

St Neot was a Saint who lived here in the ninth century — although in his story there is the possible fusing together of the lives of two Saints, one Celtic, the other Saxon. If we accept that St Neot was Saxon, then he was probably related to King Alfred who visited here and was cured of an illness by the Saint.

St Neot seems to have performed even more miracles than his fellow Saints. He had a way with birds and animals and they would often help him with his chores, but the most famous legend relates to the three fish he kept in his well. An angel promised him that if he never ate more than one fish a day, their number would never

◄ One of the magnificent stained glass windows in St Neot church.

decrease. Unfortunately, when the Saint was ill, a servant was sent to the well and brought back *two* fish, cooking them both. But all was not lost. After praying for forgiveness, St Neot ordered both fish to be thrown back and as they touched the water they were restored to life and swam happily about the well.

One of the magnificent windows in the church tells some of the legends of St Neot. These stained glass windows are world famous and arguably the finest in Great Britain. Dating from the fifteenth and sixteenth centuries, it is a miracle that they survived the depradations of Cromwell's troops.

The Civil War raged all about this tiny village which was ever Royalist in its loyalties. Even to this day an oak branch can be seen decorating the top of the church tower, celebrating King Charles' escape from the Puritans by hiding in an oak tree. The branch is renewed every year on oak apple day, 29 May.

The old coach road between Liskeard and Bodmin once ran through this village and in the slate caves to the south the navy stored their rum ration for safe keeping during wartime. These caves are now open to the public.

TEMPLE

Once the Gretna Green of Cornwall. This settlement just off the main A30 road was founded by the Knights Templar in 1120 AD as a hospice for travellers. After the Reformation, the church remained outside the jurisdiction of the Bishop until 1774 and the sixteenth century historian Carew declared, amusingly, that 'Many a bad marriage bargain is there yearly slubbered up'.

When the hangman despatched two men from this parish for sheep-stealing, in the eighteenth century, it left no men in this isolated area.

Temple is still a place that progress has by-passed and some of the buildings at the lonely Merrifield Farm are said to date from the days of the Knights Templar. The little church built by the Knights fell into disrepair many years ago, but in 1883 it was rebuilt on the original pattern. It is a stark little building, tucked away in a quiet valley and needing only twenty chairs with built-in kneelers to serve the spiritual needs of its sparse community.

TREWINT

Digory and Elizabeth Isbell put this tiny hamlet on the map in 1743, when the first Methodist preachers knocked at the door of their little cottage and asked for refreshment. They were given food and drink, and hay for their horses, faring better than John Wesley himself. He became lost on Bodmin Moor that same day and found his way to Bodmin when darkness had already fallen, only by following the sound of the church bells.

The Isbells became staunch followers of John Wesley and built a small two-room extension to their cottage for the use of John Wesley and his fellow evangelists.

The Isbell's are buried in Altarnun and their cottage still stands. Now owned by the Methodist Church, it has been restored and furnished in the style of the eighteenth century. Open to the public, it serves as both a museum and a meeting house.

Fifteenth century Panters Bridge south of Warleggan.

WARLEGGAN

The name means 'The High Place On The Moor', and although fingers of cultivated land are beginning to reach out about the village, the name is still very fitting.

Not an easy place to find, even when it has been located on a map, Warleggan is an ancient moorland settlement. One of the oldest mines on the moor lies in a wood to the north west of the village and produced tin for many centuries. Part of the workings were known by the delightful name of 'Wheal Whisper'.

This area is part of the ancient Manor of Cabilla, whose Lord held certain lands on condition that he supplied a grey cloak for the use of the Earl — later Duke — of Cornwall when he entered the county. This custom was revived in 1973 when Prince Charles was given a grey cloak at a ceremony at Launceston Castle.

**Warleggan Church — a truly moorland church
where the Reverend Densham preached to cardboard figures.**

South of the village is the fifteenth century Panters Bridge, spanning the Warleggan River. When it was found necessary to provide a wider bridge here, the council showed a commendable sense of responsibility. They built a new bridge over the river, leaving the older one to be admired by all who pass this way.

Warleggan church is very old, parts of it dating from the twelfth century. It once had a spire, but it was struck by lightning and fell in 1818, badly damaging the church.

Perhaps Warleggan is best known for the two eccentric clerics who have held this living. The first was Ralph de Tremur, in the fourteenth century. A heretic, he was accused of celebrating Black Mass in the church. The second was the Reverend Frederick Densham, the last incumbent. Quarrelling with his parishioners, he became a recluse, surrounding his vicarage with a high, barbed wire fence. When the villagers stopped attending his services, he filled the pews in the church with cardboard figures and preached fiery sermons to them. He died as he had lived — alone, found dead on the stairs of his gloomy rectory. It was his wish to be buried in the grounds of the rectory. This was not possible, but his ghost is said to tread the familiar paths that were so long forbidden to others.

Warleggan church is a splendid little place of worship, absolutely fitting for such an isolated moorland village with its stocky tower and a dipping roof made up of an uneven mixture of large and small slates. Inside, the blend of tiny windows and leaning walls completes the picture.

It is well worth a visit — if only to murmur a brief prayer for the soul of the unhappy Reverend Densham.

Legends

THE LEGEND OF KING ARTHUR

Arthur is believed to have lived during the Dark Ages, when there was very little recorded history. It would have been in the sixth century AD when he led the fight against the Saxons who seemed set to take over Wales and Cornwall.

Arthur decisively defeated his enemies and set up his famous court of chivalry, with selected knights who sat at his round table. The site of his court is hotly disputed. Some say that Camelford is the site of his legendary town of Camelot. Others put it close to Glastonbury. Tintagel dismisses all these theories scornfully and claims for itself the title of 'Arthur's Castle'.

Geoffrey, Bishop of Monmouth in the twelfth century prepared the ground when he wrote a much romanticised account of King Arthur and set him here, in Tintagel. For those who wish to follow up the Arthurian legend, there is no better place to start than Tintagel.

For the seekers of the truth . . . ? They are only the latest in a long line of searchers and will probably fare no better than their predecessors. One day, perhaps, the answer will be found — and I can think of no more likely place for the truth to be discovered than on Bodmin Moor!

TRISTAN AND ISEULT

This is an ageless love story, and variations on its ancient theme are still being written today.

Again, this is a legend from the Dark Ages, when Tristan, the nephew of King Mark of Cornwall was despatched to Ireland to bring back the Princess Iseult to be the King's bride. On the return journey one of Iseult's handmaidens accidentally mixed the young couple a love potion intended for the Princess and King Mark to share on their wedding night. Tristan and Iseult fell deeply in love and, although Iseult married the King, she and Tristan remained lovers.

After surviving many trials and tribulations, including a sentence of death passed upon them by the King, Iseult was reconciled with King Mark and Tristan went to France where he married another Iseult. Eventually, the lovers were re-united in death and buried together in France.

Although the story is no more than a legend, there is a Dark Age monolith between Castle Dore and Fowey carrying an inscription which has been freely translated as reading, 'Here lies Tristan, son of Mark'. Although not quite the relationship of legend, it is close enough to be intriguing.

We can be fairly certain that there *was* a King Mark in the sixth century and he ruled from Castle Dore, near Fowey. Some of the accounts have King Mark and King Arthur closely related. If this is so, can we doubt that Tristan and Iseult took the short route from Ireland, rather than risk the dangerous sea voyage around Land's End? Landing at Tintagel, they might have called upon Arthur and his Knights for an escort across the moor to Fowey. It is not an original theory — but an interesting one, for all that!

Some Places of Interest

BROWN WILLY

The highest hill in Cornwall is 1377 feet (420 metres). Situated in the centre of the moor to the north of the A30 road, it dominates the moorland scene. There are hut circles and tumuli on the slopes about its long-ridged peak.

CARADON HILL

The television mast rising above the tumuli and roofless mine buildings of this ancient hill can be seen for many miles around. It provides a useful landmark for those moorland walkers who are not expert map-readers.

King Charles I, accompanied by Prince Maurice, mustered his troops here on 2 August 1644 before they went on to a notable victory at Castle Dore.

Copper was discovered here in 1837, and signalled the beginning of the boom which changed the character of the eastern moor.

THE CHEESEWRING

A natural formation of much-photographed balancing rocks on Stowe's Hill, close to Minions village. From this spot there is a magnificent view over the Tamar valley to the east and open moorland to the west. Close at hand is the long-neglected Cheesewring quarry, Daniel Gumb's 'house', and an Iron Age fort. A short distance across the moor is 'the gold diggings'. Gold was found in the mines and rivers on the moor, but in no great quantities.

The Cheesewring — a favourite spot for Sunday school outings in the nineteenth century. ▶

This was a favourite outing for Sunday schools in the nineteenth century, when the children would travel here on the old mineral railway.

KING DONIERT'S STONE

At the side of the road between Redgate and Minions. The inscription, in Latin, tells us that the stone was erected for the good of King Doniert's soul. Doniert is mentioned in the Anglo-Saxon Chronicle as being a Cornish King, or chieftain, who was accidentally drowned in the nearby River Fowey in 878 AD. He is reputed to be the last Cornish King, but this honour probably goes to King Ricatus who ruled in Cornwall's far west in the tenth century.

DOZMARY POOL

About thirty acres in extent, this dark and lonely place has always fascinated local inhabitants and visitors alike. Its shores were probably inhabited before any other inland area of Cornwall. Associated with the legend of King Arthur — and the ghost of Tregeagle — Dozmary lies just south of Bolventor.

GOLITHA FALLS

Situated close to Redgate, just off the St Neot road, the River Fowey drops through an attractive wooded valley in a series of falls as though anxious to leave the moor behind. Beside the path in the woods can be seen the massive walls built in the 1850s to take the water wheel used in the Wheal Victoria Mine.

THE HURLERS

On the edge of the village of Minions. Originally the stones here formed part of three circles, erected about 1500 BC. They are

**Draynes Bridge upstream from Golitha Falls
(below) on the River Fowey**

**The Hurlers: three ancient stone circles — or
men and women turned to stone for 'hurling' on Sunday?**

probably the best known stone circles on the moor because they are
so readily accessible. Built within a relatively short time of
Stonehenge, many theories have been put forward about the uses to
which they were put. They have been variously described as places
of human sacrifice, and a meeting place for moorland chiefs. Legend
has it that the stones were once men and women, turned to stone for
playing the ancient game of hurling on a Sunday — hence the name.

KILMAR TOR

A long ridge of broken and balancing granite rocks at a height of
1295 feet (390 metres). Here is the true essence of Bodmin Moor.
Majesty, timelessness, loneliness — and sheer beauty.

KING ARTHUR'S BED

On the western edge of Trewortha Tor. The 'bed' is a huge block of stone, sculptured by wind and rain into a shape that is more evocative of a granite coffin than a bed.

KING ARTHUR'S HALL

An enclosure 158 x 65 feet (48 x 20 metres). Here and there a flat moorstone still stands to remind us that they once formed the walls about this 'building'. Its origins and purpose are as mysterious as the moor itself. It is sited on King Arthur's Downs, close to Garrow Tor — a hill with a wealth of history. Explanations put forward for this enclosure include its use as a cattle pound, or as a reservoir — hardly likely in view of the amount of water readily available nearby.

Traditionally, it is as its name implies, the hall of King Arthur. Historians pour scorn on the legend of Arthur — but it is remarkably persistent.

THE LONGSTONE

Known locally as 'Long Tom', the Longstone stands a few yards from the road, on Craddock Moor. This is just one of the dozens of similar stones scattered the length and breadth of the moor. I have chosen this particular one because its siting affords the visitor ample opportunity to stop and appreciate the atmosphere surrounding this weathered, cross-inscribed stone, 'Standing alone on a hill of storms'.

ROUGHTOR

Owned by the National Trust, this is one feature of the moor which should remain unchanged for posterity. At 1311 feet (400 metres) it is the second highest hill on the moor. There is the foundation here of a Medieval chapel dedicated to St Michael, and the remains of a Bronze Age settlement. Charlotte Dymond was murdered here in

1844 and a memorial to her stands somewhat forlornly at the foot of the slope.

Roughtor was presented to the nation in memory of those who lost their lives while serving in 43rd (Wessex) Division in the North West European campaign 1944-5.

SHARPTOR

Physically one of the smallest tors when viewed from the moor itself, Sharptor is most spectacular when viewed from Henwood village — and it is my own favourite tor. Easily accessible, it commands a breath-taking view of the whole of East Cornwall — and beyond. On a clear day it is possible to see the sea both to north and south. Originally known as Sharp Point Tor, it is distinguishable from many miles away.

Left: Trethevy Quoit — one of the finest chamber tombs in the County.
Below: Kilmar Tor: the true essence of Bodmin Moor — majesty, timelessness, loneliness and sheer beauty.

SIBLEYBACK RESERVOIR

A man-made lake, the dam was completed in 1969. Covering 140 acres and well-stocked with fish, this is a popular place with anglers and boating enthusiasts, but it is rarely uncomfortably crowded. In winter the reservoir becomes a lonely part of the moor, providing a haven for a large variety of birds, some resident, others casual visitors.

TRETHEVY QUOIT

Close to Tremar, in St Cleer parish, this is a well-preserved and impressive Chamber Tomb of the Megalithic period (2000 - 1500 BC) and undoubtedly one of the finest in the county. Originally covered in earth to form a burial mound, this tomb would once have held the body of an important member of a primitive and superstitious community.

I have mentioned here but a few of the many places of interest on and about Bodmin Moor. Lovers of the moor will already have their own favourite spots. First time visitors will find much to interest and enchant them here — and bring them back, again and again.

ALSO AVAILABLE

KING ARTHUR COUNTRY in CORNWALL, THE SEARCH for the REAL ARTHUR

by Brenda Duxbury, Michael Williams and Colin Wilson. Over 50 photographs and 3 maps.

An exciting exploration of the Arthurian sites in Cornwall and Scilly, including the related legends of Tristan and Iseult, with The Search for the Real Arthur by Colin Wilson.

'*Filled with the most beautiful photographs ... brings to life the romantic legend...*'
Desmond Lyons, Cornwall Courier

SUPERNATURAL IN CORNWALL

by Michael Williams. 24 photographs.

'*. . . a book of fact, not fiction . . . covers not only apparitions, and things that go bump in the night, but also witchcraft, clairvoyancy, spiritual healing, even wart charming . . .*'
Jenny Myerscough on BBC

LEGENDS OF CORNWALL

by Sally Jones. 60 photographs and drawings.

Brilliantly illustrated with many photographs and vivid drawings of legendary characters. The Author, who is a member of Westward Television, makes a journey through the legendary sites of Cornwall, beginning at the Tamar and ending at Land's End.

'*Highly readable and beautifully romantic . . .*'   Desmond Lyons, Cornwall Courier

OCCULT IN THE WEST

by Michael Williams. Over 30 photographs.

Michael Williams follows his successful *Supernatural in Cornwall* with further interviews and investigations into the Occult — this time incorporating Devon. Ghosts and clairvoyancy, dreams and psychic painting, healing and hypnosis are only some of the facets of a fascinating story.

'*. . . provides the doubters with much food for thought.*'
Jean Kenzie, Tavistock Gazette

MY CORNWALL

A personal vision of Cornwall by eleven writers living and working in the county: Daphne du Maurier, Ronald Duncan, James Turner, Angela du Maurier, Jack Clemo, Denys Val Baker, Colin Wilson, C.C. Vyvyan, Arthur Caddick, Michael Williams and Derek Tangye with reproductions of paintings by Margo Maeckelberghe and photographs by Bryan Russell.

'*An ambitious collection of chapters.*'   The Times, London

103

OTHER BOSSINEY TITLES INCLUDE

FOLLOWING THE TAMAR
by Sarah Foot

FOLLOWING THE RIVER FOWEY
by Sarah Foot

ALONG THE CAMEL
by Brenda Duxbury and Michael Williams

CORNWALL & SCILLY PECULIAR
by David Mudd

MAKING POLDARK
by Robin Ellis

HAWKER COUNTRY
by Joan Rendell

ALONG THE BUDE CANAL
by Joan Rendell

ABOUT LOOE
by Austin Toms and Brenda Duxbury

ABOUT MEVAGISSEY
by Brenda Duxbury

MY DARTMOOR
by Clive Gunnell

AROUND HELSTON AND LIZARD with SHEILA TRACY

HOME ALONG FALMOUTH & PENRYN
by David Mudd

THE FALMOUTH PACKETS
by David Mudd